FINANCIAL FIVES

The Top 325 Ways to Save, Earn and Thrive
to Retire before 65

Gary Grewal

www.financialfives.com

Book Layout © 2020 Daydreamz Publishing

Financial Fives/ Gary Grewal. -- 1st ed.

CONTENTS

Introduction 7

About Me..11

How to Use this Book 13

Who is this Book For?...15

Five Reasons You should Listen to My Advice in this Book ..17

Five Ways to Save Money on Buying a Car 21

Five Ways to Save Money on Car Maintenance.....................25

Five Ways to Save Money on Car Insurance 29

Five Ways to Vote with Your Wallet.......................................33

Five Ways to Identify Cheap and Sustainable Disposable Products 37

Five Ways a Zero Waste Lifestyle Will Save You Money 41

Five Ways to Professionally Vouch for a Higher Salary 45

Five Employer Benefits to Consider 49

Five Easy Ways to Save on Travel...53

Five Ways to Save on Travel Abroad 57

Five Things to Get for Free from Your Hotel 61

Five Things to Buy at Costco and Save...................................65

Five Ways to Save Money During the Fall...............................69

Five Ways to Save on Rent 73

Five Things to Negotiate with a Property Management Company 77

Five New Year's Resolutions for a Happier, Wealthier YOU .. 83

Five Guilt-Free Ways to Invest in Yourself 87

Five Ways Staying Healthy will Save You Money 91

Five Ways to Save Money at the Grocery Store 95

Five Reasons to Shop at the Farmer's Market 99

Five Ways to Save Money on Gifting and Investing in Others 103

Five Ways to Improve Your Credit Score 107

Five Ways to Protect Yourself against Unauthorized Purchases 111

Five Questions to Ask a Financial Planner 115

Five Items to Factor in when Creating an Investment Portfolio 119

Five Websites for Solid Money Advice 123

Five Financial Accounts You Should Consider Opening 127

Five Items to Discuss with Your Partner before Tying the Knot 131

Five Unconventional Ways to Save on Your Wedding 137

Five Ways to Save Money on Throwing a Party 141

Five Household Investments that will Save You Money 145

Five Items to Rent Instead of Buy 149

Five Things You Need to Stop Buying to Save Your Money 153

Five Questions to Ask Yourself before Making a Purchase ..157

Five Books to Read that will Save/Earn You Money..............161

Five Low Cost/Free Activities to do with Others (or Solo!)..165

Five Ways to Cheer Yourself Up, other than Impulse Shopping
....169

Five Ways to Save on Ski Season...173

Five Ways to Save Money on Shopping for Clothes 177

Five Protective Financial Measures to Take when You're
Young..183

Five Adult Conversations to have with Your Parents/Siblings
....187

Five Items to Keep in Safe Place to Protect Your Finances ..191

Five Ways to Save Energy at Home...195

Five Ways to Save on Utilities (Other than Energy).............199

Five Ways to Save on Your Taxes...203

Five Ways to Save on Attending a Tradeshow/Conference..207

Five Ways to Save on Festivals and Events............................211

Five Relationships to have to Save Money 215

Five Things to Look for when Considering a New City 219

Five Questions to Ask Your Realtor when Shopping for a
Home 223

Five Ways to Save Money when Buying a Home 227

Five Mistakes to Avoid as a First-Time Homebuyer..............231

Five Ways to Save on Moving Expenses 235

Five Ways to Save on Your Home Renovation 239

Five Ways to Save on the Dating Scene 243

Five Tips to Help You Manage Your Debt 247

Five Ways to Earn Extra Cash 251

Five Apps to Use that can Help You Make Money 255

Five of the Best Birthday Freebies so Far 259

Five Ways to Effectively Donate to Charity 263

Five Things to Know before Executing Your Business Idea..267

Five Ways to Raise Money for Your Business 271

Five Ways being Organized will Save You Money.................277

Five Habits to Develop to Jumpstart a Lifetime of Financial
Success 281

Bonus Section: The FIRE Movement......................................287

Five Ways to Achieve FIRE Status 289

Conclusion 295

References 297

Introduction

You're probably wondering, "What's with the *Five Ways* theme?" Well, I've read a good number of personal finance books, and though some contain valuable guidance, many can either put you to sleep or overwhelm you with never-ending stories from the author's personal experience. There wasn't a book out there that was easy to follow, concise and also packed with useful tips and advice. I consider myself somewhat of a *let's get to the point* kind of guy, so I wrote this for those who want to understand the fundamentals and go on spending more time practicing them in life.

That is the motivation for this book. Being a lifelong personal finance nerd, career Certified Financial Planner™ (CFP®) and entrepreneur, I read dozens of these books to make sure I knew all the tricks of the trade and to ensure I was doing everything right for my age. Luckily for you, I've taken all my notes from books, articles, conferences, workshops, etc., then cut out the fluff and made this easy to read book with distinct five-point chapters to help you grasp different areas of personal finance efficiently and effectively. The goal of this book is to provide you with easy to follow tips in areas of personal finance that are applicable to you, allowing you to absorb them easily and also refer back to for easy reading. I made it past $350K net worth before age 30, and you can too, with these tips. Even if you're well past your 30's and are closer to retirement rather than college age, the tips in this book apply to virtually anyone. Everyone who shops for clothes, cooks, travels, invests, gives gifts, needs care or pays for rent can benefit from this book. You're welcome!

As a young professional working in the financial planning industry, I've always felt the need to help other twenty-somethings with useful, actionable tips that will help them navigate daily life when it relates to money.

We've all been told to create a budget, and we've all been told to avoid credit card debt. Noble advice, but I'm sure you're thinking, "Well, duh, but how can I have more money at the end of the month to actually enjoy life?"

I'm here to help you with simple ideas to get ahead, financially speaking. I'm here to answer your questions about money as it relates to work, relationships, your hobbies and maybe even your retro fish tank you keep sinking money into.

You want to get ahead in life. You're ambitious, which means your money is, as well. This book is not here to act as a broken record to tell you to budget, avoid buying lattes and cut up your credit cards. It's to give succinct, dense and powerful advice in a way in which you can easily ignore the sections which don't apply to you and dive into the ones where you can really use some help. Be sure to visit financialfives.com!

About Me

Growing up in a fairly nice middle class neighborhood in suburban Northern California, I always wondered why some driveways had nicer cars than others, why some yards were more meticulously maintained and how my friends with whom I played on the street had everything from torn hand-me-down LA-Gear shoes to $120+ Air Jordan's. Then you go to high school, and everyone knows the girl who drives the new BMW or the guy with a brand-new Tacoma. Kind of funny actually, but during my junior/senior year in high school (this was right before the housing crash of 2008) we had a career day in English class, and EVERYONE wanted to be a real estate agent, as they saw their parents bringing home $50,000 a month. I wonder where those kids are now...I guess we'll see at the reunion! Wait. Never mind. Facebook has ruined any anticipation of social comparison.

Anyway, I went on to work for a full-service insurance agency, working on full commission as my first "real" job out of college. You know, the one for which you have to wear a tie and actually be on time for Monday morning meetings? Pssh...so corporate-ish, right?

After learning the ropes, getting my securities licenses and my Masters' degree in Financial Services, as well as surrounding myself with personal finance education, I felt amazed at how everything all came together to tie into real life. Before, I never knew what an IRA was or what term life insurance was. As I spoke to my friends and other young adults my age, I was surprised at how down in the dumps everyone was when it came to money, as if it was a mosquito they could just wave away as they enjoyed their organic free-range chicken avocado wrap.

Well, here we are. I've come a long way in my knowledge and experience relating to personal finance, and luckily for you this book is meant for me to share it all. As a millennial myself, I know the world we live in is a more difficult one than what our parents faced. The job market is volatile, we're being priced out of housing, you name it. I'm going to do what I can to help YOU feel confident when you snatch that wallet out of your pocket (or purse, I don't judge). Enjoy!

How to Use this Book

You'll get out of this book what you put into it, so ideally read it cover-to-cover, take notes, and read it again. Or just read a random chapter in the middle of the book and act on it. The reason for this unique formatting is to allow you to get a dose of financial wisdom with just five minutes of reading before your next meeting or while your lunch order is in the queue. Maybe you'll flip through and decide to learn about ways to save on activities this weekend. Or perhaps you're about to move and need ideas to save.

If you just read one chapter and implement the advice in it each week, look at all of the progress you will make! Don't rush through the book for the sake of completing it. The right way to leverage it is to read the content, relate it to your own life and implement the advice where applicable. Keep it on your coffee table for commercial breaks, in your messenger bag while on the train, and when you're beaming with success, gift it to someone else who can benefit from it!

Who is this Book For?

Do you receive a paycheck? Pay rent? Buy food? Breathe? (Okay, that's a stretch.) Well, then, this book is for you! This book is for those of you who have *ambition*! For those who set and keep goals. For those who deeply want to get out of debt, get a raise and live a life of purpose and prosperity, read on. However, if you're impulsive, entitled or don't care to discern your needs from your wants, you won't get the most benefit out of this book. This book is for you if:

- You are committed to achieving financial freedom
- You want your money to work for you, not the other way around
- You can visualize life when you are out of debt and ready to start living
- You are tired of paying bills at the end of each month and then having nothing to show for it
- You can't take a trip to see other places (Life's too short!)
- You're sick of missing social events due to money issues
- You are savvy in other areas of life and you're ready to get your money in order
- You just got your first job and apartment out of college and need advice

- You get the picture...

Five Reasons
You should Listen to
My Advice in this Book

So, I'm sure you're already a little dubious (you'll find that I love using hip vocab from English class) about why you should listen to me or what makes me qualified to provide advice of any kind, especially on the contentious topic of personal finance. Well that's a valid question and a perfect opportunity to show an example of the unique template of this book. Not only do I feel qualified for one pesky reason, I'll give you FIVE reasons. (Hence the title!)

My Credentials: Okay, okay, I know this isn't a resume or a toot-my-own-horn moment. (Or at least it shouldn't be. Who wants to listen to a conceited know-it-all, *scoff!*) The reason I am telling you that I have nine years in the personal finance space, have a master's in financial planning and a Certified Financial Planner® Designation is so you'll trust my guidance and suggestions in this book. After all, look at the people whose videos you watch or podcasts you listen to. Don't they have some clout in their space? Otherwise, what do they know? One slightly unsettling thing I'm seeing is many people on social media providing impromptu financial advice to strangers on forums. They may be able to tell from experience, but it's best to consult with a professional (hint!) in the end.

My Personal Experience with Entrepreneurship: I'm not going to be a broken record and repeat how everyone says it takes a special someone to be an entrepreneur. However, I will say certain characteristics of being one will make you more marketable and financially savvy. You must be willing to take risks for the chance at success. You have to sell yourself, be persistent and let the *no's* bounce off of you like a soccer ball (except *no's* don't hurt, physically at least). When I was eight years old I got my first taste of entrepreneurship by selling hot chocolate in front of my parents' house when people came to see our street's Christmas Light Spectacular, which continues to this day (the lights, not me selling chocolate). This was in an age before people had phones to Instagram my hot chocolate, but I'm pretty sure it was good, because I made more money every year until I entered high school. Then at 23, I started a reusable moving box company, California Box Rental, because I saw how wasteful moving can be with cardboard, as well as not being very protective for your possessions. I learned to be organized, creative with no marketing budget and how to get partnerships with other businesses, but also I learned budgeting, initiative, delegation, public speaking skills and many other traits which can serve you well in your career, as well as apply to a variety of personal financial topics.

Devouring Personal Finance Books and Articles: I've probably read close to 100 of these books, and a gazillion more articles on Money, Kiplinger, Inc., and other magazines with topics on personal finance and investing. As you'll find out in this book, I *love* to read. For me, nothing is more peaceful than diving into a book, not even yoga or hiking (mayyybe getting a massage or hanging in the hot tub, but that's beside the point). Whenever I read a book or an article which I find resourceful, I always have a little notebook to write down notes in, to make sure I take the most valuable guidance or knowledge to improve my own situation. Why do you care? Because it takes hours upon hours to read all these books, digest their content, write down the most compelling points and organize them into thoughtful advice in my own words, some of which I will share with you in this book.

Giving Advice to Others: I've been in the financial planning industry full time for more than eight years, and guess what I have been doing all that time? Providing personal financial advice to clients. In this book, you're the client. Except as a bonus, I am giving you all the other advice I think is useful that I wasn't necessarily able to give in my positions because of regulatory restraints (and maybe due to the fact that I needed to keep my opinions out of any engagements and be impartial all the time). I've helped clients who are just starting out and trying to get out of debt, young clients who feel uncomfortable with a sudden inheritance, clients worth millions who want to give it all away and others who just want to know the difference between a Roth IRA and a Traditional IRA. This book is my tell-all, my big dish-out, my genuine and wholehearted attempt to use all the knowledge that has benefited me and spell it out in easy to read content for you.

My Exposure to the World of Personal Finance: In addition to reading tons of books and articles on personal finance, I've also meticulously combed through blogs, online forums, classes, videos, as well as attended many presentations, conferences and events around financial planning to feed on the information that may not be widely known, but has been provided to the privileged or those who want more than just to retire at 65 and pay off the house before they are dead. I've been in conversations discussing compelling strategies and insider advice which I generously share with you in this book

Five Ways to Save Money on Buying a Car

Okay, so you're tired of puttering along in that same 1996 Honda Civic with which you picked up your Homecoming date in your senior year of high school. How do you even begin? Well, first you need to narrow it down to which car you want, what options you want/can live without, your budget, etc. Once you've got that down and have taken a few cars for a spin, it's time to get down to business. My preference is to deal with a private party to avoid dealer markups, but luckily for you, I've got experience in both.

1) <u>**Buy Toward the End of the Month, and if You Can, at the End of the Year:**</u> You may know that when new models come out and leases are returned, the used car market is usually more flexible, which means more selection and a better price for you. If you're really daring, go into the dealership on a Sunday evening during unpleasant weather when they're hungry to meet quotas. If you are there with money in hand, they will bend over backward for you. Make sure you come with evidence of comparable models elsewhere. When I did this, I paid $3,700 under the invoice for the car!

2) <u>**In General, Go for Certified Pre-Owned, (CPO)**</u>: However, if you can get a lower price, tell them to throw out the certification. The car should have been thoroughly inspected, cleaned and will have all maintenance up to date, so you are getting a CPO car without paying for the flashy certificate. Then, ask the dealer for all service records and a multi-point inspection, which will come in handy when you decide to sell the car for a higher price. This is because of the CPO seal that you never paid for in the first place!

3) <u>**Ask for Freebies**</u>: Sometimes, dealers have gone as far as they can (or want to) go in reducing the price. So, ask for one year of free service, oil changes, free tires, free 60,000-mile service, a year of free car washes, car mats or window tinting. Get creative. Dealers can usually do many things in-house at a lower cost, so they may be more flexi-ble in this area. I got the last dealer to mount custom wheels for me, free of charge!

4) <u>**Know how Long a Car has been on the Market**</u>: Generally, a seller will be more eager to unload a car the longer it has been for sale. You can see the date it was posted for sale in the fine print at the bottom of the Craigslist ad or on the dealer's

website. Then, make sure you ask for service records and a history report to make sure it's a good buy. Is it an off-color? Is it a convertible and you're looking in January? Are gas prices super low and it's a hybrid? Knowing what is going on in the market can be an asset for you in buying a car.

5) **<u>Buying New? The Internet is Your Friend:</u>** If you're set on buying a new set of wheels, you have another option that can save you big bucks. Now, I'm a huge advocate of buying pre-owned and letting someone else take the hit on depreciation, but if you're stuck on being able to customize your ride and shun away the secondhand cars, then try sending offers over the Internet. Let's say you want to buy a new Toyota 4Runner. Most likely, there are a handful if not dozens of dealerships within 50 miles of your residence. You can use cars.com or go onto each dealer's website, as they usually have an Internet sales department or a *Make an Offer* button. Tell them exactly what you are looking for and for their best price, or make an offer, and then copy and paste that request for the other dealers. Now, sit back and wait for the best offer to come in. If you're feeling really lucky, forward the best offers to the others and pin them against each other. Make sure before you go in

that you ask about any other fees for which you would be liable, as well as any other incentives being offered.

Five Ways to Save Money
on Car Maintenance

Here is a secret: Not everything a car dealership says you need to do is accurate. Now, I'm no car aficionado. However, most independent auto technicians will tell you certain factors of a 30K or 60K mile service are excessive, especially if you take good care of the car. In any case, car maintenance costs can add up, so here are some ways to hold onto your green.

1) **<u>Buy a Reliable Brand:</u>** There is a reason some car models are no longer on the road and why some brands such as Pontiac have disappeared completely. If you're not a car person and are just buying off the *cool* factor, be sure to do your research. MSN Autos, Car and Driver and Consumer Reports are all great sources when it comes to not only looking at expert ratings for reliability and such, but also reviews from actual owners. By purchasing a reliable brand, not only will you most likely save money on repairs and maintenance, but also, the resale value of your car will be higher. There is a reason Honda and Toyota beat out so many other brands for resale value--they last forever!

2) **Negotiate Maintenance into the Purchase if Buying from a Dealer:** Unless you're a guru of negotiation, you're probably not going to get your neighbor Bob to pay for oil changes for a year after buying a car from him. Buying from a dealer, however, is different, as they have more flexibility, especially when buying new. As you may recall, I don't recommend buying a brand-new car simply because of the obvious immediate depreciation, but there are many pre-owned cars on the market. If you can't get the dealer to move on price, ask them to throw in a warranty or free maintenance for a year or three. Or how about all maintenance up to and including the 30,000-mile service? Now, asking them to buy you brand new tires might be pushing it, but choose your buying time carefully and you may just find all kinds of deals thrown at you just to get you to buy the car. Some dealers will also provide a student discount, a military discount or even a loyal customer discount. Ask, and you shall receive!

3) **Don't Go for Flashy:** Most luxury brands not only cost more to maintain, fuel and insure, but also to service. A friend of mine owns a BMW, and he paid over $500 for an oil change service! Now, there

was a water pump or something broken, as well, and he'd also spent about $2500 on non-oil change repairs and service since buying the car just over a year ago. Granted, it does have almost 100,000 miles on it. Go online for yourself and you'll see that an oil change for a Toyota Corolla is about $30, but for a Mercedes E350 it's about $150-$200! Also consider that you will need tires, brakes, alignment, timing belts, batteries and other services. That's not even including if you need a repair to something such as your electrical system or air conditioner.

4) **Learn Some DIY:** I know, I know. You're probably thinking, *What? I have to actually open the hood? I thought that was like mechanics-only territory?* Well, let me just say you don't have to actually change your own oil, since that's pretty cheap just to get done at the dealer or a local shop. Other things, such as learning how to jumpstart your car, change the battery, top off fluids, put air in the tires and change a tire are simple things you can do without dropping unnecessary cash. Pick one or two things you can picture yourself doing and leverage the generous YouTube video creators who have content on learning how to do some of those things on your own!

5) **Use the Competition:** Okay, this is where it gets fun. A good amount of a dealer's business comes from the parts and service department. While most dealers will match their competition, you'll want to check with yours to see what the parameters are. Does the competitor have to be within a 100 miles? If you drive an Acura, can you use Honda coupons? You can do a simple online search to see which car dealers of your brand are local to you. For example, if you drive an Infiniti and you live in Phoenix, AZ, do a Google search with that information and then click on the maps section to find them clumped within the metro area. Once you get to the website, most dealers have a *Service Specials* page. Even if you can't find a dealer with a special for the particular service for which you are looking, look for general coupons such as *15% off service of $100 or more or 25% off service of $200 or more.* Some geographic areas also have dealer associations, such as Northern California Acura Dealers. They will usually have a list of all the dealers in the group in case you want to cross reference your Google search.

Five Ways to Save Money on Car Insurance

If you're intent on owning a car, insurance is a must, but that doesn't mean you have to overpay. If you're in a policy just because you signed up with the agent who sponsored a table at the home and garden show you went to with your parents, check out these tips.

1) **<u>Go with an Association such as AAA:</u>** AAA is one of the largest insurance companies. I have found their rates to be pretty competitive with the coverage offered, as they are a nonprofit. Geico and others may be a better value, as well. If you have multiple cars, you may get a discount. If you have homeowner's/renter's insurance, boat insurance or even life insurance through them, you may get a break. Even my science degree from undergrad got me a discount! Plus, associations usually produce an annual dividend, and since they are nonprofit, those are returned to policyholders such as you and can be used to further reduce your premium.

2) **<u>Comparison Shop Online:</u>** Remember those websites mentioned, such as bankrate.com? There are

a growing number of websites which can provide quotes for finding online quotes for insurance. Again, check with your alumni association, employer corporate discounts, Costco or even a collaborative shared workspace group to which you belong. Be careful not to just fall for a low price. Be sure you are accurately comparing coverages and how far each coverage extends.

3) **Ask for Discounts, even those not Posted:** Many companies offer discounts such as good driver, no accident, multiple policy, multiple vehicles, etc. One strategy is to fill out a quote and continue almost to the point where you purchase coverage. At that point, the company may realize you're a validated customer and they won't want to lose you. Ask the rep what other discounts they can provide. I was able to find a discount by telling the agent my car has vehicle skid control, backup sensors and keyless entry. You may also find a low mileage discount, a mature driver discount, a student discount or an alumni association discount. Remember the saying *ask and you shall receive!*

4) **Don't Duplicate Coverage:** What I mean by this is don't pay for an aspect of coverage you may also receive somewhere else. For example, if you have

short-term disability through your employer, don't pay for additional coverage through your car insurance policy. Your credit card may already provide coverage for a rental car, so there's no need for extra coverage. Or maybe your homeowner's or umbrella insurance policy covers medical or property damage for another party, so check to make sure you're not paying for that, either. Higher deductibles help, too, and you can sock away the savings in an investment account to cover the difference in the slight chance you need to cough up the deductible when applying the insurance coverage.

5) **Pay Annually:** When you owe money on a premium, most companies would rather you pay annually upfront as it cuts down on their administrative costs, rather than processing your payments on a monthly or quarterly basis. I have seen an itemized line item on statements of a friend's policies where $7 a month is added to the premium when it is broken down and paid monthly. That's $84 a year down the drain! Easy money to save by simply paying it once a year and being done with it. Another bonus is you don't have to worry about a late payment affecting your credit or adding late fees because it's all done.

Five Ways to
Vote with Your Wallet

Hopefully, this is a starting point for helping you live out your values and principles by choosing from which companies you buy your products. We are fortunate to have so many choices and a plethora or information to help guide us to put our money in companies that believe in what we believe. FYI: I don't have any relationship or receive any endorsements from the companies I list in this book. I'm just providing suggestions based on my research on what companies believe in living above their bottom line.

1) **Buy Local:** If you can't resist buying oranges, watermelon and summer squash all throughout the year, whelp, can't help ya there. Large produce companies transport goods all over the world. Some grow their commercial products in environmentally degrading ways. Many of us know the detrimental effects of climate change and understand reducing trucks/cars on the road is one answer to the problem. So, mix up your weekly routine and go to the farmer's market for fresher, healthier and better-tasting produce with an increased selection. Besides, they always have super

good samples and other cool booths. It's like a festival every week!

2) **Support the Little Guys:** Instead of buying Brawny paper towels or Scrubbing Bubbles cleaning supplies, you can opt to go for greener, less chemically intrusive products from companies such as Method, Seventh Generation or Green-Shield Organic. These products are usually made out of recycled plastic and plant-based ingredients. This goes from everything from your body wash to laundry detergent, as all of those chemicals drain into our water supply one way or another. Oh, and ditch the store-brand cleaning products. There's a reason they are cheap and have long warning labels!

3) **Boycott a Company:** Don't like the Koch Brothers anti-climate agenda? Don't buy Georgia Pacific products (toilet paper, napkins, etc.), and look to the companies above that provide that, too! Did watching that farming documentary on Netflix open your eyes to food giant Tyson Foods? Start buying alternatives such as Mary's Chicken or Applegate Farms. Keep your eyes and ears open, especially in regard to larger or regular purchases, for companies that may not jive with your values.

If engaging them in the issue you have doesn't resolve anything, let them know of your decision to stop supporting them and follow it up with action.

4) **Create a Following:** Sure, if you've already got a substantial following on social media, your public outrage about a company could float you some clout in making a change. But if you don't have this power, you can still do things such as purchasing email distribution lists, ads on social media or have radio/podcast hosts share your message online. Now, this book is all about being fiscally responsible, so don't go out and buy a billboard. However if you have earmarked funds for charitable giving or activism and feel passionate enough to direct your energies and resources this way, buying an audience, followers, or publicity may help you feel more in control of where your money goes.

5) **Remove Your Spending from all Companies Associated with the One in Question:** In this day and age, many large companies are owned by a larger parent organization or are involved in some way in a complicated conglomerate. Even small companies whom you thought were independent may have been bought out by a large organization. Think Talenti to Unilever, Justin's to Hormel, and

RXBar to Kellogg. If you think a clothing company should be banned because of the way they source their products or treat their workers, boycotting that brand will send a signal, but ceasing the purchase of all the company's other products, as well as those of the parent company, will send an even louder message. Procter and Gamble, Unilever, Kimberly Clark and many other publicly traded companies oversee many everyday brands you may use in your daily routine. Want to take it even further? Find out who the suppliers of those companies are. What is the end product? Where do they source their raw materials? What transit companies do they use? Thinking big picture, especially with supply chains, can help your efforts to truly vote with your wallet.

Five Ways to Identify Cheap and Sustainable Disposable Products

I've done comparison shopping and can tell you there is not always a major (more than $1) price difference between environmentally friendly products and conventional ones. I've bought 100% recycled aluminum foil and Method plant-based all-purpose cleaner for under their conventional competitor prices. So, here's to saving money AND the Planet!

1) **Check the Packaging**: You probably know by now to avoid name brands and to check the store brands. Don't be afraid to check out new brands, either. If you don't like it, the store will usually accept it back. Make sure it says something like, *Made from 100% post-consumer recycled material* or, *Made from recycled bottles.* Also, what is the quality of the packaging? Can it leak or be easily dented? Or is it opaque to skew how much content is actually in there?

2) **Read the Ingredients List:** Does it look as if it was made in a biohazard lab, with ingredients such as oxybenzone or formaldehyde? Make sure it says something like, *plant-based"* or *biodegradable,*

something along those lines, so you don't start losing your hair or developing eczema while you wash your car or clean out your garage. Also, just my humble opinion, but there's no need to pay extra for organic non-edible items such as organic coconut milk in your hair conditioner.

3) **Read the Description for Information:** How many ounces does it have compared to other brands? Sometimes the package will have a blurb about the product or company. This is usually where it will mention it is a sustainable product with no animal testing and fair-trade, etc. This is a good sign. You want to use products that are good for your body and good for the items for which you are using them. If you use a wood polishing product with quality ingredients, your expensive bar stools, entertainment center and coffee table will last much longer and may potentially fetch higher resale values if you someday move out of town. If you use cheap, harmful or abrasive ingredients, you may end up replacing those items. Have you ever faded your leather couch by using some powerful *all-purpose* cleaner?

4) **Made in the USA?:** The more products you buy that are made closer to where you are, especially food

and body care items, the less of a carbon footprint it leaves behind. Tell the store you shop at to locally source more products, and that may even end up driving down the price! If products come from afar, they may have to pay extra for shipping, which consequently costs you more. While products made in the U.S. are typically more expensive than those made in China, you should also weigh the quality of the items.

5) **Look at the Company's Responsibility Policy**: If you are loyal to a particular brand, check out the manufacturer website to see how they practice CSR, or *Corporate Social Responsibility*. Check to see if they take the effort to publish a Sustainability Report, so you know for sure when you give them your money they are doing the right thing. This will make you feel more in control of how you vote with your wallet, what your money influences, and also if the company uses profits to more drive down prices for you rather than compensate shareholders and executives.

Five Ways a Zero Waste Lifestyle Will Save You Money

You may not have paid much attention to buying wrapping paper that's just going to be torn and tossed. Buying $3 bottles of water at the convenience store (or $8 for one at a stadium--yes I saw it!). Buying a tube for a spur of the moment ride down the creek, only to shove it in the garage after you snag it on a rock. These are examples of purchasing things items that are both wasteful for your wallet and our pristine home environment. The closer you get to Zero Waste, the more $$$ you save!

1) **<u>Avoiding Overconsumption:</u>** Pay attention to things you don't need. Dryer sheets, paper towels, bottled water, pre-cut melon in plastic tubs, and much more. Food waste is a big drain on wallets. Up to 40% of the food we buy doesn't end up being consumed. What a waste! *Buy-two-get-one-free* strawberries--will they get moldy and be tossed out? Next time you go to a party, look at how people fill their plates and then leave half of the food untouched. Talk about indulgence and waste! Pay attention to what you consume, make use of leftovers and freeze what you can.

2) **Reducing Costs of Disposables:** So you bought three cases of bottled water for $10. What a deal! Until it's not, and you have nothing to show for it after it's gone except garbage. A few of the disposables you can skip include bottled beverages, coffee cups, sandwich/freezer bags, cleaning wipes, napkins, plastic flatware and plates, serving platters, Q-tips, and the list goes on. Take inventory of what you shop at the store for (besides food) and see if you can replace those items with reusable options such as cloth napkins, glass/plastic food storage containers, cotton cleaning cloths or a reusable bottle/thermos.

3) **Less Space/Storage:** Remember back in the day when you went to a friend's house to play or your band practiced in the garage, and it was always full to the brim of *stuff*. You probably just never gave it any thought, and many of those items pretty much died a slow death when your parents decided to have a garage sale or move. Americans love their stuff so much that we have a multi-billion-dollar self-storage industry which is pretty much just a spillover from people's homes. According to an April 2015 article on the Huffington Post, the U.S. has substantially more storage

centers than it does McDonalds! You see those shiny bikes at the store or get jealous when you're neighbors always go kayaking, so you get your own, the dog gets tired of his bed so you stash it, and before you know it, every closet and bit of free floor space in the house is habitat for items that are sparsely used anymore, if it all. The less junk we buy, the more we simplify our lives and focus on experiences, not things, meaning we need less in our lives. The less we need means less storage space, and possibly can enable us to move to smaller homes or apartments, which may translate to big savings.

4) **Decrease Tendency for Impulsive Purchases:** When you strive for a zero-waste lifestyle, you'll learn to turn a cold shoulder to eye candy that really doesn't matter anymore. Have you ever gone to a home and garden show and bought that cool wind chime because you had to have it, or to a community festival where aggressive exhibitors sell window dressings, antiques, garden accessories or trendy kitchenware? Or just think about when you go mindlessly shopping on a trip or browse online when you're bored. When is the last time you went to Target and ONLY bought shampoo and toilet paper because that was all you

needed? "But that countertop mixer will make me want to bake all time," you say. Never happens. By spending your money consciously and knowing what does and what doesn't bring true value to your life, you'll save a bundle on junk that just doesn't fit your lifestyle.

5) **Saving by Making Your Own:** This one requires a little more time and effort but definitely involves some saving. For example, you could make your own cleaning products with baking soda and few other ingredients or make your cleaning cloths by cutting up old shirts. I've even made my own dryer sheets by rolling small pieces of cloth into a jar half full of water and half of fabric softener. Now I'm not saying go take sewing lessons and buy fabric in bulk to make your own clothes, but you may consider starting with things as simple as making your own coffee or gardening your own fruits and vegetables and then progressing to making your own coffee table from an old door. Check out this nifty link from BuzzFeed on what you can make so you can save the money for things you love. https://www.buzzfeed.com/peggy/household-products-youll-never-have-to-buy-again-792?utm_term=.leqY94p5N#.bxd0JaWkD

Five Ways to Professionally Vouch for a Higher Salary

So, you're finally on that pedestal where an offer has been extended. Congratulations!

You may be so excited to have a job, you'll say yes to whatever they throw at you. Don't--at least not in a healthy job market. In my experience, you have the most leverage to get a higher salary in the time between when an offer is made and accepted. The company has made an investment in time and money in recruiting you (especially if they had to fly you out) so know they are interested. Sure, there are countless ways to save money, as you'll see in this book, but getting a raise is one of the few ways to make a lasting and considerable bump in your income. Here's how to get the biggest boost in a starting salary in a professional manner.

1) **Know what You're Worth:** You need to know what others are getting paid in this position with relevant experience and qualifications. Ask around, check online at sites such as salary.com, and know the range. Know if they pay more for certain designations, licenses, certifications or other experience that makes you more valuable to that

specific company. There is nothing worse than accepting a position out of excitement, only to find out later most others in your position are earning more simply because they asked for it or know the right people.

2) **Prepare a Counteroffer:** Have you ever been jealous when an ex wound up with someone else, especially if that someone else was a rival? Well this is like that on a less dramatic scale (hopefully). When you've got other options, you've got more leverage to negotiate, because the recruiters are now in a position where they have to win you over from another company. Try to know the hiring timelines of the companies with whom you are interviewing ahead of schedule so when your prospective employer makes an offer, the others make them around the same time.

3) **Set Yourself Apart:** Even though you meet the job qualifications, point out what you have done in your previous roles that set you apart. Perhaps you have a Masters' degree, a certain designation or certificate. Always have specific examples and statistics of successes you have had in the responsibilities the role asks for. Also, anticipate the questions you will face. Research these online, on

forums or in alumni job boards. Be sure to know about the company values, why people work there and other notable facts. Roleplay your interview or practice in the mirror. Just as you want to brag about yourself, you also want to impress the interviewer regarding what it is about that company that compels you to work for them.

4) **Show Them how You will Add to Their Bottom Line:** No one wants to hear an entitled person list why they deserve more money, but when you position it in a such a way that you will make the company money or reduce expenses, well, now, you've got their attention. You can demonstrate what you will do that will add value and ask for a commensurate increase. For example, if in your last job you lead a project to increase the efficiency of an HR process or created an imperative software program used by the travel and events department, talk about how much this saved the company in money, improved productivity, reduced overtime or eliminating the need to hire an outside vendor to troubleshoot the problem. This is real money that can be in your pocket instead of some miscellaneous expense account.

5) **Give Up other Perks:** If you plan to bike to work, ask them to waive the parking/public transit stipend. Tell them you don't want the wellness reimbursements if you work out at the gym in your apartment complex or if you have other options. Do you have insurance through a parent or spouse? Tell them these benefits are appreciated but you would rather see it translate to a higher salary.

Five Employer Benefits
to Consider

There are surely more than five perks if you have a large or fairly generous employer. Even if you are self-employed, some coworking spaces offer similar benefits and discounts and cool perks such as social events, free coffee and snacks, etc. For the most part, however, this section is about more than just the standard benefits of retirement plans, fitness reimbursements and commuter benefits. Take 30 minutes to scroll through your HR page or ask a HR specialist for 10 minutes of their time to explain things to you if you didn't get the full scope when you were first hired on.

1) **Employee Assistance Program:** These are often referred to the acronym EAP. Employee Assistance Programs may be anything from legal assistance, grief counseling, marriage or personal counseling or alcohol/substance abuse assistance. One company I know of provides up to six free sessions with a therapist for each issue on which you are working (depression versus the burden of caring for a loved one), plus the benefits cover everyone in your household. If you look at what

some therapists or counselors charge on their own, they are not cheap. Some charge more than $150 an hour or per session. What a wonderful resource to allow yourself to divulge your struggles or frustrations in your relationships, career or financial situation. Talking to others, especially when they are just doing their job, can help you think through life's biggest conundrums and help you get back on track to health, wealth and happiness.

2) **Corporate Discounts:** The three employers I have been with after college so far have all provided some sort of discount program for employees. Granted, they were all national companies, so if you work for a local paint shop this might not entirely apply. Check your HR page or with one of the specialists. While these discounts may not be extravagant, they can save you some serious cash. $25 off monthly gym membership dues, 10% off dry cleaning services, BOGO free pass to area attractions and museums are all discounts I have seen at one time or another. One time a coworker told me about the discount our employer provided for personal--not business--car rental. I had no idea, and it cost me less than $30 to rent a car for the day. I also found out through the company's real estate

portfolio that several hotels were available to us at 50% off the market rate. Vacation anyone?

3) **Educational Reimbursements:** The cost of tuition this last decade has many people shaking their heads at why they jumped on the boat of higher education. You should absolutely invest in yourself if it will help you achieve your goals and prosperity later in life. But if it's going to cost you $70,000 to get an MBA and you barely have $5,000 in savings, it may not be the best to blindly take that dive. Many employers want to retain key employees and offer incentives not to jump ship (liking these maritime references?), so they may offer tuition reimbursement up to a certain amount or even pay for the whole degree. You may have to work for a year or so to be eligible, and they might also pay for certifications and other licensing you need to move up in your line of work.

4) **Wellness Counseling:** This refers to things such as weight loss management and nutrition consultations. What does this have to do with saving money? You'll see in a whole chapter devoted to comparing good health to saving money. You can work with a dietician on crafting a meal plan that works for you or just vent about your lack of

willpower to avoid donuts and ice cream every Friday. They will listen to your situation and provide a roadmap to getting healthier. They may also provide their own tips on saving money at the grocery store, restaurant or with food preparation. It's not all about gagging on quinoa and kale. Give them a shot and find out for yourself how creative you can be with your snacking and meal plans.

5) **Subscriptions:** You should already know, this being a personal finance book, I'm probably going to denounce signing up for a magazine, newspaper or some doorstop meal prep box. Libraries are gold in my view, as you'll find out. Some companies offer free individual subscriptions to things such as the *Wall Street Journal*, *TIME Magazine*, or professional associations related to your work, such as the *Association for Financial Professionals*. The latter can provide additional benefits, with discounts to coveted professional development opportunities.

Five Easy Ways to Save on Travel

I recall a memorable trip to Pittsburgh PA, and I have to say I am seriously considering moving there. Three rivers hug a vibrant downtown with impressive bridges crossing them, and picturesque nature in all the right places. If you've never been, now's your chance to catch a Steelers game! There are a few things I learned on this trip which may help you save money on your next adventure. Many young adults are travelling to check out new places to settle down, interview for a job or maybe just take in new experiences. Here are ways to accomplish that and feel good about your bank account when you return.

1) **Join a Hotel Rewards Program:** Sure, you could jump on Airbnb or shack up in a hostel, and these are excellent options. However, if the idea gives you jitters and you want a clean, secure place to grab some Z's, joining a rewards program from Hyatt, Marriott or other chain will make you appear more loyal in the hotel's eye. In addition to getting points toward a stay, you can score free breakfast, free parking, free wi-fi, and preferential room choices. It's also easier to bring up concerns about

your stay which may translate into more free stays.

2) **Consider the Train:** This is a good option if you are not in a time crunch. What I've found is that if you take the train (Amtrak), you usually arrive at your final destination in the morning and can sleep in the seats overnight. They're actually quite comfortable. The train is the way to go, especially if you want to hit up multiple cities on a route. Plus, unlike airports, the stations are usually in city centers, so you don't have to pay for a shuttle or taxi to get somewhere.

3) **Fly if You're by Yourself; Drive with Friends:** Just do the math. It usually works out in your favor to split the gas a few ways when driving. Be sure to add tolls, parking and food. If you're flying by yourself, try to fly on Tuesday, Wednesday or Saturday for cheaper fares. Now again, it depends on what kind of trip you are looking for. If you just want to spend a long weekend in Seattle, don't feel obligated to drive to save money. You may have to take more time off, and if you feel tired after all that money, you might need another vacation, anyway. On the other hand, if you want to see many places along a route, such as when driving from

Boston to Washington D.C., then it may make sense to drive. The other reason to drive is if you are not just hanging out in a city, but driving to state or national parks, beaches or mountain towns, where long distances and little-to-nonexistent public transportation can hamper your ability to move around.

4) **Don't be Scared of Public Transportation:** When I went to Chicago, Vancouver, Phoenix and a few other places, I found taking the light rail or express bus was much cheaper. Rather than paying $60 or $70 for a taxi (or a little less for Uber/Lyft), I spent around $2-$7. Plus, you get to explore some points of interest along the way and get a feel for the locals there. Strike up a conversation. Most people are happy to share places you should check out, overrated attractions, tips or insider tricks to getting tickets/reservations to a sold-out event or neighborhoods to avoid. I've also found mass transit to be more enjoyable, as you can spend your ride planning your next outing or just looking out the window to get a feel for the city. No need to find/pay for parking, either. Also, buy a pass on your arrival/departure dates, as you can usually get free transfers throughout town and then to the airport/train station.

5) **<u>Actually Visit the Visitor's Center</u>:** I get that you don't want to look like the fanny-pack flaunting tourist. But the staff there are usually really helpful regarding the top places to see and the best times for festivals, events, etc. You can also find discounts and freebies for restaurants, activities and nightlife. In addition, you can also get a solid opinion on a place you wanted to check out which perhaps you found on TripAdvisor.com to see if it's really worth it or if there is a cheaper attraction to better suit your needs. Think of the visitor center staff as your travel concierge. They are really helpful!

Five Ways to Save
on Travel Abroad

Yes, travelling abroad gets its own spot on the list, because you're dealing with different languages, currencies, laws, rules, customs, etc. It's helpful to have a friend who is from or familiar with the area to which you are travelling, but with tools like TripAdvisor.com and other sites you can find out the essentials relatively easily.

1) **Have a Zero-Fee ATM Debit Card:** This is very important, as depending on where you travel, most vendors prefer cash, and you'll most likely need to pay in their currency. As you may already know, small business owners pay a fee for credit card sales, so you might save money here, too. You never want to be in a situation where you only have your credit cards, and the cab driver, clinic or hostel host won't accept it. Whether you're going to a coffee shop, hole in the wall bar or farmers market, having a zero-dollar foreign transaction fee card can save you loads. Chase Sapphire and Capital One seem to be top of the list. Check them out: https://www.nerdwallet.com/blog/top-credit-cards/no-foreign-transaction-fee-credit-card/

2) **Be sure to have Travel Insurance:** This may end up costing you about 5% of the total cost of your trip, so it might appear to be total waste. These days, there are so many types of insurance--pet insurance, phone insurance, hoverboard insurance, even pizza insurance. (I literally just saw an ad that says you can buy insurance in case your pizza gets messed up on the way from the restaurant to your destination. What has this world come to?) On a more serious note, a sudden injury or illness for you or a loved one can derail your trip. Sure, some airlines offer travel funds and some hotels have a 24-hour cancellation policy. However, many still do not, especially for international travel. Some travel businesses don't reimburse for adverse weather, either. Before you go out and buy travel insurance, see if your credit card company offers it as an additional benefit, as many do these days. Otherwise, check with your current insurance provider, asking if they can throw some in, before you resort to a web search.

3) **Look into Extended Layovers:** As you may know with domestic travel, sometimes booking two one-way tickets rather than a non-stop, or one with an extended layover in a city, can be much cheaper than a direct flight. This may especially be

the case if you are flying from a smaller city, say Tucson AZ, to Brussels. Not only can separately booked flights or those with a longer layover be cheaper, you can save on lodging costs, as well. Instead of arriving at 9pm at your destination with a direct flight, maybe you'll arrive at 9am the next day, taking a red-eye flight the final leg of the trip. Sure, you may be a little tired to go all out adventuring the day of your arrival, but the excitement of the realization you're on vacation and saving money should more than compensate! In any case, you'll sure sleep solid once you have an actual bed.

4) **Travel Light:** This should come as no surprise. If you can avoid paying baggage fees, why not? It's not just the airlines to and from a foreign country that may charge you baggage fees. Think of the travel you'll do in the interim on trains, busses, ferries, taxis and on foot. The more you have, the more likely it is that you'll be charged. Also, that's one more piece of luggage you have to drag along with you, and one more to keep an eye out for from thieves. If you can carry it with you, you're also less likely to pay for storage fees or tips for bell service. Some hostels and smaller foreign airlines also limit what you can bring, so avoid trouble

and try to truly embrace the "backpacker" lifestyle!

5) **<u>Check out a Travel Guidebook from Your Library:</u>**
I recommend borrowing rather than buying travel
books because you'll probably have no use for it
after your trip, and it's a better use of resources to
pass that book of knowledge to the next adven-
turer. If you haven't noticed by now, I'm big fan of
libraries. Not only are you saving money by borrowing the book, since it is free, you'll also find lots
of insider tips and useful information in that book.
Sites to see, places to eat, more ways to save
money, common phrases in the local language and
resources for help if you ever run into trouble. Libraries typically loan books for about three weeks
and generously give renewals, so it should be
plenty of time to use it and return it.

Five Things to Get for Free
from Your Hotel

Now, to add to the savings of travel, we come to the wonderful world of hospitality. I absolutely love hotels. The service, the thoughtful gestures, the music, the design and the relaxing feeling of just sitting in the lobby enjoying the surroundings. I visit some hotels when I'm not even staying there! When you are, though, here are opportunities to stash your cash and stretch those hotel reservation dollars beyond just a free breakfast (too easy).

1) **Sewing Kit:** Ever have that moment when you're on a business trip and you pack your best dress shirt, or maybe staying for a destination wedding and you brought your favorite skirt, only to notice a tear or a missing button? *Gosh*, you think to yourself, *all that time I was planning to wear this.* Sweat not. Ask the concierge or the front desk for a sewing kit and you'll have a thread and needle in no time. Why waste money and time going to an alterations shop? You can keep it in your travel bag, as well, in case you rip your sleeve closing the overhead bin.

2) **Shaving/Toiletries:** You're probably thinking these are a given. I'm not saying to grab all the shampoos and bars of soap if you don't need them. However, if you forget something beyond the basics (toothbrush, toothpaste, floss, shaving cream, razor, deodorant, even a comb) just ask the front desk. Chances are, they'll have extras for guests who forget them. ASK (see the recurring theme). If you're polite, they may even give you some things for free that they normally sell, such as sunscreen, lip balm, laundry soap, etc. Just because it's not in your room by default doesn't mean they don't have a stash in the lobby for that extra resourceful guest.

3) **Maps and Travel Guides:** While much of this is available just by going online, you may find yourself with a poor signal, strained eyes or a dead phone battery. Or maybe you're tired of switching between nine applications just planning out your morning. Many hotels will have maps with a lot more detail than your phone contains, and the staff can typically offer suggestions on getting to your stop, as well as highlight the path or nearby landmarks, saving you time and frustration. You may have seen magazines such as *Where* or local

publications telling you about the hottest restaurants, best places to watch a sunset or scenic bike trails. Some of these magazines which are placed in your rooms or available at the front desk even include discounts and coupons for various tours, attractions, landmarks, and more.

4) **Transportation:** It may be anything from a shuttle that only goes a five-mile radius from the hotel to full-on car service on demand. Take advantage of these, especially in city centers, tourist areas or near airports where taxis and Uber can be quite pricey. Always check the website of the hotel to see if this is an option, and if it is not explicitly listed, read the reviews or call the front desk. It may be that the shuttle is only available during certain hours, or car service only for Platinum-level guests. Doing a little research can not only save you money and time, but also enhance your experience (wouldn't you rather ride in a Tesla than a Crown Victoria?) Apart from cars, some hotels I have been to also check out bikes, beach chairs, umbrellas, longboards, scooters and roller-skates to guests, free of charge!

5) **Event Tickets:** Okay, so you're not going to get suite level seating to a Broncos game (most likely).

However, you may score free entry to a matinee, a movie screening, a baseball game or a carnival. Depending on the hotel where you stay, some concierge desks have valuable connections with event promoters, concert organizers, club managers, etc. You can benefit just by asking or looking through the services guide in your room. When I stayed at a Fairmont Hotel in Vancouver, they offered free cover to a popular club plus a free drink. In Las Vegas, where connections are a premium, you can often get onto a guest list of a coveted club simply by asking the concierge. Another friend of mine received two free tickets to the Portland Art Museum as a peace offering for having his room ready 20 minutes later than expected.

Five Things to Buy
at Costco and Save

I know what you're thinking. Why would you want to go to the zoo they call a warehouse store where people shop like it's Black Friday every time you go there? I've shopped around a good amount, and I can assure you these are the five best things to buy at Costco versus other stores. The best part? If you're not happy with your product or it doesn't work out the way you wanted, they have a very generous return policy. So go ahead, buy that planned purchase with confidence and ease of mind.

1) **Clothes:** No joke. I can buy everything from brand name boardshorts to dress shirts at least 30% cheaper than at another store, even when I have a coupon or there is a sale elsewhere. Hurley, Kenneth Cole, Calvin Klein and The North Face are all brands I have seen there, so you can be sure you are purchasing quality. Next time you're in the market for a pair of jeans, check out Costco and I think you'll be pleasantly surprised. Their buyers sure have an eye for selection and finding items that are hot sellers. It's especially good to buy those clothes that are more for utility than

fashion, such as socks, undergarments, under-shirts and gloves.

2) **Cleaning Supplies**: Think about it--cleaning prod-ucts don't really spoil or lose effectiveness when stored, so instead of shelling out $5 for a little bot-tle of dish soap, you can get a good eco-friendly bottle twice the size for maybe $1 more. Dish-washer detergent, laundry soap, napkins, multi-purpose spray or whatever you use can be bought for cheap and stored, and they sometimes have good coupons on them. Make sure to download the Costco app or snag a coupon book once you walk in.

3) **Dry/Canned Goods:** Oatmeal, nuts, almond butter, pancake mix, chia seeds and especially protein powder are bargains at Costco. Wait for a coupon on these babies and you may save around 50%, even more if you usually buy this stuff straight from the gym or nutrition shops. Considering a bag of whey protein is usually around $40, that's a pretty decent savings! As long as you have the storage for it, buying dry goods will save you in the long run. Or you can share it with a friend/room-mate who doesn't have a membership.

4) **Gift cards:** Whether you find yourself frequenting Jamba Juice or The Cheesecake Factory, or you just need a gift for the wedding next weekend, you can usually pay about $70-80 and get $100 worth of gift cards. Instant save! I believe these circulate throughout the year and also include some local places depending on where you live, so don't ignore this if you don't care for chains. There are massage and gym membership gift cards, as well. Just be careful who you give these to.

5) **Kitchen Gadgets:** Not only does Costco usually carry a high-quality selection, but with a coupon you can usually save $30 or more. Say you want a standard blender. It's $100 at Bed, Bath and Beyond, $80 at Costco, and with the coupon it's $55. Win! Now just because kitchen gadgets are cheaper at Costco doesn't mean you need them. Are you really going to start making your own bread, ice cream or coffee if you purchase these items? Be realistic with yourself. Set a budget, and if you commit to using it, then buy it.

Five Ways to Save Money During the Fall

The sentiment here is meant to channel your creativity to save during each season, but making you read four chapters on saving money during various seasons would be overkill. Fall is also a great time to take a look at where your money was spent in the summer and also reflect on what your goals might be for the coming year. I'm going to take this time to give you some ideas on conscious spending on popular items for fall.

1) **Garbage Bags:** If you're lucky enough to have a yard, you're also lucky to get to rake all those leaves. The best thing to do is to dump them into your green waste bin if your city provides one, or at least put it into a compostable trash bag you can usually find at Target, or better yet, a reusable, machine washable trash bag such as *Eco Trash Bags* (think of all the $$$ you'll save). Oh, and don't even think about buying a polluting leaf-blower. Raking is good exercise and it doesn't require fuel.

2) **Partywares**: As the season goes from backyard BBQs to indoor potlucks and parties, not everything will be finger food (no judgment here!). It's

best to go with real dishes and silverware to avoid wasting money and disposables. However, I understand throwing a party can be exhausting. When shopping at Whole Foods, Sprouts or your usual store, look at the bottom of the package for 100% post-consumer recycled content, compostable or some sign that it is eco-friendly. Or to go cheap, try the dollar store, or see if friends, neighbors or community groups who've recently had an event have any leftovers. Make it fun by creating nicknames for your party guests and writing on cups and even plates to avoid waste. Feeling festive? Check out this cool site: *Eco Party Time*

3) **Halloween Costumes and Candy**: I'm not one to contest tradition. (I used to trade all my candy for peanut butter cups, because that's all I wanted.) However, buying heaps of individually wrapped candies is wasteful and way not original. Remember that garbage bag dress and duct tape couple at the homecoming games? Put your imagination to work, maybe throw in some oranges, pens and pencils, rulers, school supplies, juice bottles, or even put some finger food on a platter and hand it out to avoid packaging and wrappers all in front of your place. Heck, even throw in some floss to

balance out the evil. Quality, not quantity, my frugal friends.

4) **Start Shopping for Summer Clothing:** Board shorts and flip flops are on clearance. Take advantage! You can even look up a product online, and since many clothing stores price-match, you'll get an even better deal (unless they have a clearance-price only type policy). There are cool websites that suggest when to buy what. I haven't validated everything, but feel free to check out this list from LifeHacker: http://lifehacker.com/5973864/the-best-time-to-buy-anything-during-the-year

5) **Plan or Go on a Vacation:** After asking dozens of hotel concierge professionals, I've learned that during the fall, travel slows down. Whether kids are back in school for families or convention/conference season is winding down, you can use this chance to capitalize on the low demand! Do some research on which destinations are offering the most price cuts and you might find yourself enjoying a platinum-level vacation for college-student prices!

Five Ways to Save on Rent

The last time I signed lease in my apartment complex, boy did it taste bad. I've been fortunate enough in the places I've rented. I just paid for rent, the utilities were paid by the landlord and I never had to sign anything more than month-to-month.

Well, now I'm dealing with property management companies and it's much more complex. I feel as if their lease agreements are more like contracts to buy a house--they are THICK. Anyway, without further delay, here is what I've learned through the process and what you can do to save on housing.

1) **Scope out Rooms for Rent/Sublets rather than Single Apartments:** Usually, people who are on a lease need to fill an empty room and are much more willing to be flexible on rent/lease terms than a deep-pocketed property management company. Of course, this may work best if you are single and don't mind living with roommates, but you save $$$!

2) **You can Still Find Deals Downtown or by the Beach:** Yes, if you can live outside of the high demand areas, go for it, as you will likely have much

nicer amenities for the same or lower price. That being said, you can find deals in desirable areas by getting more roommates, signing a new lease during the winter, taking a unit without a view, balcony or lower floor, or even signing a longer lease if you will be in the area for a while.

3) **Take Tangible Evidence with You:** Whether you meet with an individual landlord or property management, know what the going market rate is for the place you are looking for. Find comparable units that are cheaper and possibly have better amenities, and the leasing consultants may be more willing to cut you a deal if they see you are knowledgeable. They may also have wiggle room worked into their budgets for securing residents, so you might be able to get the application fee, administrative fee, transfer fee and any other ludicrous and useless fees waived like I did. I've also found it's easier if it's a new building they're trying to fill up, or if it's a complex where new competition recently sprouted up. You can also use an apartment locator service and ask what the financial incentives are for working with them.

4) **Schmooze with the Current Roommates:** This works if you are dealing with an individual

landlord. When I moved to Orange County, The landlord was asking $850, and I got her down to $750. How? I made friends with the roommates when I was looking at places and told them why I was a great roommate. In turn, they vouched for me to the landlord. If she can have a responsible, clean person with whom the others get along, she would rather take my price and not deal with the hassle of a problematic tenant.

5) **Get Renter's Insurance:** Not only will this protect your belongings if a pipe bursts or the place goes up in flames, but it will usually get you a discount on your auto insurance if you bundle it together, and the landlord may provide you with a discount because you are transferring liability from them to an insurance company. Some places now even require it. The best part? It is usually around $10 a month, less if you pay annually (which I always recommend if you can afford it because you avoid pointless service charges).

Five Things to Negotiate with a Property Management Company

I could never quite put my finger on it, but I always disliked property management companies. They serve a vital purpose in ensuring multi-family complexes operate efficiently and safely. However, my experience with them is once you sign a lease, they are more inclined to serve the owner than the tenant. So, the way to feel better about the fact that you are paying them is to pay them less.

1) **Application/Administration Fees:** I have paid an application fee before, but only because the apartment was a really good deal and I convinced my roommate to pay $300 per month more for the larger room. I've never paid administration fees, though. I firmly believe they are bogus. Sure, an application fee costs the property management company as they have to run a credit check, but they paint the administration fees as paperwork preparation and all that. Well, guess what? The leasing staff is there anyway. I'm not going to pay them an administration fee. This one is usually pretty easy to ask for them to waive, as long as you play the game right in how interested you are in

the apartment and are on the cusp of signing a lease.

2) **Transfer Fees:** Let's say you move into a one bedroom, but then you and a friend decide to move in together to save some money. Good job! Be careful, though, as the management company of your apartment complex may slap a transfer fee on this request, and I've seen them as high as $600. Ideally, you want to ask what the transfer fees are before signing a lease with a place, but let's say you overlooked this. Respectfully approach the manager in the leasing office and explain your situation. Maybe even offer to sign a longer lease. Or you could use this as an opportunity to bring up issues you have with your current apartment, such as the noise through the walls or any other aspect of your tour that didn't exactly measure up. Instead of getting a bad review or an unhappy resident, they might make the decision to waive your transfer fee to keep you a happy, rent paying resident who just may refer others. Speaking of...

3) **Referral Bonus:** When you live in a major metropolitan area, especially downtown where they are lots of multi-family complexes competing for your money, referral bonuses abound. Next time you

look at a complex's website or on tour, keep an eye out for a referral bonus. Try emailing the leasing agent about it so you can have evidence of how it applies. Generally, it only works if you refer someone and they sign a new lease on a different apartment. What my strategy was, I was planning to renew my lease, but gave my 60-day notice anyway to see what they would do. First, they offered to cancel the rent increase. Then, since I had to find a new roommate, I told them I wanted a referral bonus as I would be referring someone to sign onto the lease with me. They reasoned that it wouldn't apply as I was just getting a new person signing onto my lease, not a different apartment. I told them the only reason I was going to re-sign my lease was that I referred someone to the complex and they decided to sign on with me, so essentially the apartment complex got a new lease out of it. They made the exception and I got a $1000 rent credit. Ask, and you shall receive!

4) **Free Rent:** Let's say you are planning to sign a new lease and the apartment complex is offering *free rent for a month*. Ask what lease term it is for. Typically, it is going to be for a longer lease term, such as 12 months, so they can lock in getting that income and justify losing a month's rent to prevent

sooner turnover. Or maybe they are offering one month free and free parking for three months if you sign for 15 months. Just because it isn't written doesn't mean it doesn't exist. Think about how long you plan to stay in the area and maximize your lease to say, 18 months. I know someone who did this and negotiated getting one-and-a-half months free, three months free parking and $1000 in gift cards! And then, 10 months in when he wanted to change his living arrangement, he posted the room on Craigslist and got someone to take over the remaining eight months. While this is risky if you don't intend to fulfill your lease term, many people would love to take over your lease from you if they can sign on for just six-to-eight months, as they value flexibility.

5) **Deposits:** When you sign a lease, whether for a home or an apartment, you're typically asked to put up a month's worth of rent as a deposit, in case you mess up the place, get laid off and can't pay rent or just ditch your lease. These days, with so many damage recovery options for landlords and multi-family buildings, you should be able to ask them to waive the deposit, even if you have a pet. They key here, as with many other points made, is having evidence from competing

properties. Or make a case to the property manager that it's the last thing preventing you from signing on the dotted line. The other thing to consider is attempting to look for a brand-new or newer building. Usually they are aggressively trying to fill up the empty units and are willing to do what it takes to sign someone on for a year or more.

Five New Year's Resolutions for a Happier, Wealthier YOU

You may not be reading this around New Year's, but why buy into resolutions around some arbitrary date? Sure, it's easy to brush money issues off for when you get that higher paying job, when you pay off your loans or when you get an inheritance. It's great to have a plan for what you will do when certain milestones are reached. However, you can always start creating better habits now that will pay dividends for many years to come. Well, being a personal finance author for young professionals, here are my tips for a solid year!

1) **Set up Automatic Transfers:** I can't emphasize this enough. Not only does it save you time, but automatic transfers ensure you stay on track for your savings goals, as well as having your bills paid on time. You can put away 10% of your paycheck into an online savings account each month on the 2nd, along with your Roth IRA contributions, while all your credit cards can be paid on the 5th or whenever your billing cycle closes. Then, use a tool like mint.com to check your transactions once a week and make sure everything lines up. When you don't have a chance to spend money that you

never even see, it becomes a whole lot easier to live within your means.

2) **Get a Bike or Light Rail Pass:** Most of us millennials live in cities or urban areas where we don't need to drive to every single destination. I ride my bike a mile to work every day, even when it snows, although, I probably end up walking to avoid a wipeout. I see people paying between $12-$18 every day just to park their cars. That's up to $4,500 a year on parking! If you don't like biking, try public transit or carpooling. You'd be surprised to find your work benefits may have some kind of commuter benefit that pays for a monthly pass. Plus, the time you spend as a frustrated driver can now be spent reading (a personal finance book of course), socializing or listening to music. Also, many cities have a free metro service for weekdays to get around the inner downtown. Check out your regional transportation provider's website.

3) **Don't Sign a Full Year Lease if You can Help It:** Each city is subject to swings in rental rates based on demand, so try to sign a shorter lease and don't let them slap you with surcharges--plenty of places do this. If you can't, at least try to sublet through

someone or take over their lease. Then, when prices change, you can be ready to let the leasing offices feed you grapes and shower you with deals to get you to sign. Or, if you're settling down, look into buying.

4) **Learn Basic Investing Principles:** No one is going to care more about your money than you. Besides, have you asked yourself what all of this is for? Why are you working? Why are you saving? Know the answers to these questions. Then, go to the library and check out a few investment books. Also, check out some great sites for learning such as www.investopedia.com, www.bankrate.com, and www.morningstar.com/cover/Classroom.html.
You should be able to understand why asset allocation, rebalancing and low fees are important in designing your portfolio. If you don't understand something, don't invest in it.

5) **Become a DIY-er:** If you're 25 or 30 and you have a cleaning service for your place, I'm going to come over and hand you a broom. Seriously, unless you're making six figures and absolutely cannot handle cleaning your kitchen, you should clean your own place. It takes an hour or less per week, and you can make it fun by putting on music or a

timer to see how fast you get done. Other things you can do yourself include ironing your clothes (look at the tag--dry cleaning may not be necessary), painting a room, cooking, washing your car, and more. If you're a hands-on person, consider teaching yourself how to install a new lighting fixture or change your oil. Not only will it save you money, it'll give you a fresh sense of self-satisfaction!

Five Guilt-Free Ways
to Invest in Yourself

Warren Buffet famously said, "The most important investment you can make is in yourself." I couldn't agree more. Your biggest asset is, well, YOU! Your ability to learn, earn and grow throughout life. Now, don't go running out on a shopping spree or apply to Ivy League schools to get another two degrees just yet. Adhere to this list, young lad, and you will know some ways to best grow as a person.

1) **Work Out and No Junk Food:** As much as you hate hearing this, listen up. You can't be the best version of yourself if you're overworked, stressed out, sleep deprived, while also being a couch potato and living off frozen entrees. Get on a workout schedule, make food at home, or at least make healthier choices out and stick to a regular sleep schedule. Try it. You will feel so much better. I used to work out a lot, run and play tennis, but still eat things such as pizza, pasta, cookies and fries regularly. When I changed my diet to primarily fruits, veggies and proteins, I felt so much more robust and energetic. More energy = more productivity = more money!

2) **Get Schooled:** If you're stuck in a low-paying job you hate, it's time to hit the books again. Don't sweat it. If the thought of going to school again terrifies you, there are tons of credential and license programs with flexible schedules, online classes and affordable courses. Your community college is a great place to start. Think hard about what you enjoy and what your skills are and then do some research on in-demand jobs in our area. This can be anything from an Auto Mechanic to a Water Treatment Technician. These jobs are in demand, the outlook is good and you're making a direct impact on the world instead of shuffling papers in some big office every day.

3) **Read, Learn, Repeat:** The most successful people in our country, as busy as they are, still make time for reading. It's exercise for your brain, will sharpen your understanding of the world around you and will improve your vocabulary. Not only that, it's a FREE way to have fun while also building your human capital (library anyone?). You can read books about getting along better with colleagues, building furniture, how governments and companies operate and of course how to improve your finances. Getting a library card may be the best decision you make for yourself. Who knows? Maybe

you'll start a side business of making greeting cards from plants because you read a book on it. You're welcome.

4) **Grow Your People Network:** Just because you are not looking for a job doesn't mean to stop networking. Those you meet and surround yourself with can mean anything from a dream opportunity, to a well-positioned mentor, to just a new friend. Think about who you would invite to a dinner party if you could bring anyone in the world. What qualities do these people have that make you want to be around them? Getting out there and strategically meeting new people may accelerate your career, get you more customers, introduce you to a field you're passionate about or even get you connected to the company you've been vying to break into. Volunteer at events and conferences, go to professional happy hours, business -oriented Meetup groups or even seminars on topics that interest you, from fashion to sustainable finance.

5) **Dress for Success:** This is the one time it's okay to spend money on clothes and grooming--but don't get too crazy. You still need to save and budget for it. There is substantial research on how others

judge a person based on how they look, usually within 20 seconds of first meeting. Going off the last tip, if you go to a networking event wearing a plaid shirt and skateboarding shoes, it's time to invest in your appearance. Have at least one outfit you would wear to your dream interview. Little things like a tie clip for guys or a necklace for ladies can make a great first impression and command a higher degree of respect. Keep your shoes clean. Keep your clothes ironed and pressed. Get your haircut from a barber, not your 14-year-old cousin. Invest in a good watch, cologne/perfume, grooming materials, and other accessories relevant to your lifestyle and job. Not only will you earn the respect of those around you, you'll garner a higher level of confidence!

Five Ways Staying Healthy
will Save You Money

So, you think just because you're in your mid 20's you can live off burgers, beer and weekends full of raging bar hopping with little sleep? Well, maybe you can. But if you want to have the energy and vitality to live a prosperous life, you've got to prioritize your health. Plus, you'll save money! Here's how.

1) **Health Care Costs:** This is the biggest, perhaps the most obvious one. The unhealthier you are, the more likely you are to end up in the hospital or under a doctor's care. Most of us have seen our premiums increase as employers look to push more of the costs to employees. If you are healthy, you don't need to see the doctor as often, hence less co-pays, hospital bills and specialist invoices. Ask a few seniors who are on an oxygen machine or walk with a cane what they wish they'd changed in their lives, and I bet some of them would wish they had taken better care for their bodies.

2) **Less Money Spent on Prescriptions, OTC Medicine, and Supplements:** I can't believe how many

people I see shelling out $30 to $40 for supplements such as Omega 3's or multivitamins. If you just include fish, fruits and veggies in your diet regularly, you'll be fine. And then there are those who think they can eat Cheetos and cheese steak sandwiches all week and then buy diet pills. What's the point!? You're just sabotaging yourself. Do you really think it will be that easy? As any healthy person or personal trainer will tell you, balance your diet and exercise. Abs are made in the kitchen. Lastly, the healthier you are, the less you will spend on medications from the big pharmaceutical companies. We all know what a bargain those are.

3) **You'll Save on Travel:** We all know that most airlines will make you pay for an extra seat if you "spill over." However, also consider that if you are healthy, you'll have no problem walking about a city instead of taking a taxi. You'll also be in a position to bike around town, whether it be to work or the grocery store. Thus, parking, fuel and transit costs will decrease.

4) **Save Money on Unhealthy Products:** Smoking can cost you $5,200 per year or more, according to Investopedia.com (The Real Cost Of Smoking by Michael Deane | June 19, 2009). This includes

everything from cleaning costs to lost opportunity. Consider when you walk into a sales
meeting or interview smelling like a chimney--will
it jeopardize your success? You bet. It's not just
smoking, either. Alcohol costs can add up fast, especially if you are spending $100 on drinks every
weekend. And don't even get me started on frozen pizza.

5) **Save Money on Services:** If you are healthy and
able-bodied, you can do your own laundry, clean
your own house, garden, wash your own car,
move, cook your own meals and even do your own
DIY projects. This can be anything from building a
bathroom cabinet to installing a ceiling fan. If you
are injured, have low energy or are just not in the
shape to do these tasks, you'll have to pay someone to do it. Labor is one of the most expensive
costs. Think about all the things you pay someone
else for and how much satisfaction you would get
from doing them yourself--hence saving major
moola. Not only can you do many things yourself,
but you can make money doing them for other
people. There are a plethora of apps to walk dogs,
house sit, run errands, etc.

Five Ways to Save Money at the Grocery Store

Ah, grocery shopping. That exciting time of the week where we can stare at that gelato in the freezer section and declare, "I deserve this!" Or we test our willpower by strolling by the bakery section. There are literally hundreds of items screaming for our attention and money. So, how do you save money when your eyes just want everything?

1) **Make a Meal Plan:** Ever open your fridge to find those blueberries growing some mold, or that bloated almond milk carton that you only used half of? Making a meal plan will help you make sure you don't waste food and thus money. It may take you a week or two to determine what portions you go through and what you can freeze or use into other dishes. So make it fun! When you prepare your meals for the week and find you've got some spinach or bell pepper left over, whip up an omelet or side salad. Most produce can be readily frozen, as well, so you can save it for another meal when you're running short on some ingredients.

2) **Shop during the Middle of the Week:** Many times, grocery stores run specials during the week, and sometimes they overlap in the middle of the week when a new circular comes out. Plus, shopping during the weekend may increase your urge to buy that cheesecake or that innocent little tub of gelato for movie night. Hey, you've had a hard week, it's the weekend, what's wrong with a little treat? Stick to your plan! If you really want to reward yourself, save the money you spend on those frivolous store-bought treats and visit your favorite eatery for something special. A bonus for sticking to your meal plan during the week.

3) **Spoiled Food? Return It!** How many times have you opened up that box of organic strawberries or that tub of spinach, only to realize fungus or mold has sadly taken the life of your beloved grocery item? Make sure you select the package with a *best-buy* date as far out as you can, but even then it should last a few days longer. Most grocery stores will happily exchange the product for free if you take it back or bring in your receipt. That adds up when you buy $5 baskets of berries and salad. See this quote from the USDA: "*With an exception of infant formula (described below), if the date passes during home storage, a product should still*

be safe and wholesome if handled properly until the time spoilage is evident."

4) **Skip Beverages:** How much is that organic cold-pressed beet and cucumber juice in your hand? Oh, did you want four of them? Guess it's between that or the dinner party this weekend. The best beverage for you is water, and it's free. Forget anything bottled. I will say if you consume cereal or tea, maybe look into some nut milks (pint sizes are less expensive, and you don't have to worry as much about waste). If you love fancy drinks, juices, wine or whatever else, make it a treat. Take a friend out to celebrate her new job or take a buddy out for a draft beer just because. You'll save so much money by passing on the bevies.

5) **Forget the Ready-Made Stuff:** I know, you think there is no way you will have enough energy to cook after work, never mind packing your own lunch. You pass by that delicious-looking Tuscan chicken pasta and pesto veggie microwave meal, thinking, "I deserve this! I'm too tired to cook, anyway." Look, you pay for convenience. Ever notice how the cut watermelon is way more expensive than just buying a watermelon? This goes back to my first point. Meal plan for the week. It won't be

easy at first and you may want to give up, but you WILL save money, taste fresh food variety during the week, be healthier AND develop confidence and appreciation of your blossoming cooking skills. TV dinners are so 1995.

Five Reasons to Shop at the Farmer's Market

Okay, this is going to make your Saturday mornings worth getting up before 10am, so listen up. You want to eat healthier? Help the environment? Tired of plastic-tasting produce from the supermarket? Farmer's markets are becoming increasingly popular across the country. Just a quick Google search will direct you to one in your neighborhood. Reasons I love them include:

1) **The Freshest, Best-Priced Produce Available:** Did you know that fruits have seasons? The reason you see everything at the store is because it comes from all parts of the world. In my opinion, fruits not in season lose their taste. And oranges coming from New Zealand to New York are bad for the environment. Go to the farmer's market and you'll find juicy peaches in the summer, persimmons in the fall, and some fruits and veggies all year long! A bountiful harvest during the applicable season will also usually mean lower prices due to copious supply.

2) **Direct Producer to Consumer:** The guy putting my nectarines in a bag is the same one who cultivated the soil and harvested them. That's love. And it tastes sooo good. I don't know about you, but I'd rather not eat a zucchini from 1,500 miles away that was picked a month ago. Plus, I've found that if you buy a few items, are a regular customer or come toward the end of the day, they'll throw in extra stuff for free or slash the price.

3) **No Pesticides, No Wax:** The produce here literally looks as if it was taken from the ground, and with good reason. The farmers are not mass producers and they take greater care in the development of their produce. Being that it was recently harvested usually means it will hold its flavor and last longer. That means you won't waste money by having spoiled food on your hands. Plus, fewer pesticides and whatnot is better for your health, and we all know how that saves you money.

4) **More than Produce!** I've found cashew butter, cookies, mango salsa, beet pesto, spicy sweet potato spread, lavender ice cream--you name it. Talk about impressing everyone at the potluck. They'll never find your secret ingredient at the store! Plus, you're supporting local entrepreneurs and your

community economy. Think outside the box? You may find your next business idea or partner with the creativity at the farmers market.

5) **<u>Free Samples, Sunshine, Music and Food Trucks:</u>** Just more reason to make it a weekend ritual and get a good vibe start to your week/weekend! Like I said, you never know who you're going to meet, and being in an environment like that can also make you happier and more productive later. Besides, attending the farmers market and buying produce beats a trip to the mall to buy full-priced clothing you don't even need.

Five Ways to Save Money on Gifting and Investing in Others

Ever get a gift from someone that you just know was regifted? Maybe the fact that it's a product that isn't even on sale anymore, or they gave you a home spa kit when you don't even like taking baths. Regifting is great if you have something you don't want or can't use, but someone else can and they have some kind of engagement coming up. If you really want to stand out, though, consider these gifts that not only will save you money (not competing with others) but leave a lasting impression, as well.

1) **<u>Donate to a Charity for a Cause They Love:</u>** This is my favorite one because it goes above the materialistic gifts most of us give and receive for life's celebrations. Charity was not talked about much in my house, so now that I am aware of all these deserving charities that truly have a track record of success, it is hands-down one of the most fun things to spend money on and feel good about. Share that feeling with your family and friends! Is your nature-loving bestie getting married? Get her a membership to the local land trust. Maybe she'll get info on exclusive volunteer events, hikes and a

magazine covering all her favorite things about nature. She will remember this long after the wedding as it keeps on giving, unlike that $300 crystal vase she has no use for in her urban Chicago apartment. You get a tax-deduction, you help out a good cause and strengthen a friendship! One website to check out is tisbest.org. It allows you to make a charitable donation and let the recipient pick their favorite cause!

2) **Get a Gift Card for Something They are Dealing With:** Is your friend so busy they can't cook but they love a certain type of food? Did they go through a stressful time at work or at home and need a massage? Do you know if they could use new tires on their car? Not only does this show you are paying attention to them, it will pay dividends to their well-being later, and they have you to thank for it. You can save on gift cards by (here it is again!) purchasing them at Costco. For example, get a $100 Massage gift card for $79.99. You can also scope out sites such as CardPool (https://www.cardpool.com/) to find unwanted gift cards sellers are offering on the cheap. These sites are also great if Aunt Marjorie got you a gift card for DressBarn that you would even feel guilty regifting.

3) **<u>Give the Gift of Time or Connections:</u>** Is your friend or cousin far away from home and a little lonely? Maybe a trip to visit them would mean the world. This can double as a gift as well as vacation for yourself. Or maybe your uncle lives two hours away and you drive out to take him to lunch. Or the neighbor wants a job at the art museum, and you know the director--introduce! Maybe your neighbor is tired of working overtime and you invite them over for dinner and surprise them with a few days' worth of premade meals to ease the burden. (Warning: only do this if you are a good cook!) Think of it this way--if you're needing to save money, time spent with people you rarely see is sometimes all they could ask for. In this era where we all have our headphones in and our faces buried in our smartphones, a little love and warmth in connecting can go a long way.

4) **<u>Put your Handy Skills to Use:</u>** Maybe if it's your dad's birthday, instead of buying him a rotating tie rack and yet another watch, you can clean the gutters of the house, wash and vacuum his car and organize his desk. Sometimes, dads are so busy taking care of household finances, working and other tasks that a little help can go a long way,

much more than some static gift, because you put time and effort into it. Maybe you're good at technology. So help a friend build their website. Or you can invite your cousin over for some cooking classes. Why not even help your mom with home and financial record organizing? Maybe it's on the to-do list but feels overwhelming. Use your skills!

5) **Buy in Bulk:** If you intend to attend a dozen weddings this year or want to strike out gifts for all your friend's kids' birthdays, you may consider buying gifts in bulk. Let's say you want to buy five his-and-hers bathrobes for the weddings this year. You can approach the retailer with a request for a discount because you are buying a few of them. Restaurants, theaters and event centers also tend to offer discounts on certificates bought in bulk (Buy two $100 gift cards, get a $50 gift card free, which you can use for that friend with whom you never really felt close ;)

Five Ways to
Improve Your Credit Score

Your credit score is probably a lot like your asset allocation strategy--you don't actually realize how important it is until it's too late. From buying a house, applying for an apartment, a credit card or a business loan, you need a good credit score not only to get approved for a loan or financial transaction but to receive a coveted low rate. The better rate you receive, the more money you save!

1) **Don't Close out Old Accounts:** Old debt that you have paid off is good for your credit scores, because one factor of your credit score is the length of time accounts have been open. This is especially important when you are just starting out. Just because you don't shop at Macy's anymore and have paid off that account, you may not want to close it anytime soon if you are relying on a healthy credit score, such as when buying a car or a house.

2) **Set up Automatic Transfers to Pay off Full Monthly Credit Card Balances:** Generally, this only works if you have a healthy spending habit, as in not spending more than you make. This is because you can't pay off a credit balance if you don't even

have that much money in the bank. And don't even think about paying for one card with another--this rarely leads to financial discipline. However, if you stay within your means and are conscious about your spending habits, setting up automatic payments can ensure you never incur a late payment or carry a balance, two large impacts to your credit score. Most major card companies will allow you to set up automatic payments online and will email you statements and confirmations so you can always keep tabs on your finances. I monitor my *mint.com* transactions weekly, as it tells me when certain card payments have been submitted and also lets me cross reference what was charged and if the totals are journaled correctly.

3) **Don't Carry a Large Balance:** Setting up automatic transfers should take care of this problem. However, there are sometimes exceptions. Let's say you just bought a vacation to Italy for $3,000 on the third of April and your statement does not close until the 1st of May. Well, that $3,000 is going to linger on that account for almost a month until your automatic payment rolls around. To avoid the negative hit on your credit, any time you have a large purchase like that, go in and manually submit

payment or wait until your statement is about to close to make these kinds of purchases.

4) **Don't Open Accounts at the Store just to get a Discount:** Sales associates at retailers often are incentivized to open new credit accounts for customers which is often accompanied by a, "You can save 25% off of your purchase today!" Don't go for it. You should carefully research and select which credit cards work best for your lifestyle. Do you value cash back? Travel mileage? Perks? No annual fee? You can research which cards are best for your current situation at sites like *nerdwallet.com* or *bankrate.com*.

5) **Know what Your Card Limits are and don't Push It:** Typically, your credit score is partially determined by how much revolving debt you have access to versus how much you are actually using. According to *bankrate.com*, you should aim for using up to 30% of the amount you are allowed. Make regular purchases on your accounts, and don't consistently carry a $4,000 balance when your card has a limit of $5,000. If you have good payment history with the company, you can typically call them or go online and apply for a higher limit, which will help if you tend to run over the 30% rule.

I have done this in the past and they have raised the credit limit just by asking. Again--ask and you shall receive!

Five Ways to Protect Yourself against Unauthorized Purchases

There are few things that offend me financially as much as seeing either my credit card information compromised or an unscrupulous vendor trying to take advantage of my patronage. I'm a finance guy, and if there is one thing you don't mess with, it's someone's hard-earned money. Luckily, with most transactions occurring via credit card, you can both track purchases for proof as well as leverage the large credit card companies to dispute transactions on your behalf if it gets to that point.

1) **Make Sure Your Credit Card has a Dispute Process:** This is a must. Fortunately, most cards do have this program free of charge and will go to bat for you when problems arise. However, always check and read the fine print in this area. Understand that process. Is it user-friendly? Do they require all documentation before they even acknowledge it, or do they first make the vendor prove the charge was valid? My card company has a very easy process on their website. You login, find the transaction on your account activity and then just click *Dispute this Transaction.* It's a three-step process to say why you are disputing the

transaction and to upload any documentation. The rest is in their hands, and they'll put a conditional credit back on your account until the claim is resolved.

2) **Document Everything:** I don't mean just keep receipts. When you dispute a service, for example a yoga studio membership you thought you'd cancelled, make sure you get a copy of the written cancellation request you'd submit to them or any email from one of the associates that they have received your request. Most vendors have requirements that you must cancel a recurring service several days before your next billing date, so be conscious of this, as well. If you are disputing a product you feel is subpar or something along those lines, document the emails exchanged with the vendor, transaction numbers, dates, photos of the item, etc. You want to make it as easy as possible for your card company to fight the charge on your behalf, and documenting everything you can is the best way to do this.

3) **Try to Talk to the Vendor First:** As with many conflicts in life, sometimes just having an honest conversation with a company/vendor with whom you are unhappy can rectify the situation. These

days, with online reviews and social media, businesses know how quickly their reputation can be damaged. Be honest, respectful and rational in your quest to recover the charge or get a replacement. Rather than deal with intimidating card company representatives or risk bad reviews, businesses may just do what it takes to keep you as a happy customer. It also helps to buy from reputable companies and online sellers, so you know others have had good experiences as well, and they will make you whole if need be.

4) **Have Your Card Issuer Send You a New Card:** If your card was stolen or you keep getting unauthorized charges, the best thing to do is to get a new card issued with a different card number. If your card was stolen, this will stop the thief from adding charges to your account, and if reported in time, most card companies will relieve you of responsibility to pay for the unauthorized charges. If the card is being charged for a service you cancelled or are disputing, this will prevent the vendor from being able to keep charging the same card, since a new card will have a different number. A new card is a fresh start, and free, so take advantage of it!

5) **Set Reminders for Cancellation Periods:** As mentioned above, most companies or subscription services have cancellation periods, usually 7-10 business days prior to the regular billing date, to prevent your card from being charged again. Look up all the services you currently have, such as gym memberships, dating services or magazines and create reminders in your phone or a note next to each vendor in your budget so you don't have to worry about remembering those dates, which almost never happens (at least not for me). As soon as you know you are moving or you no longer need a service, look up these services and know these dates. Or if it is a sudden event, reference point #3 above in talking to the vendor about your situation.

Five Questions to
Ask a Financial Planner

A financial advisor can be incredibly influential in your life, so it's imperative to do your homework if you decide to hire one. You will probably have more than five questions for someone with whom you are trusting your life savings. Hopefully, however, these are some of the more pointed ones that will help spark new questions as you attempt to decipher if the individual you are considering is worthy of being on your payroll.

1) **How are You Compensated?** The last thing you want is your advisor making tons of money off investments that are not really in your best interests. *Do you receive any commissions? If so, how and on what products? How does that translate into the advice you give me?* Ask what the fee schedule looks like and if it depends on your net worth, the amount of investments. What kind of breaks are available? Another way they may earn money is not by fees, but by the percentage of your assets under their management. That way, they'll make more money only as your account increases in value. If you only want financial planning, check out fee-based or retainer-based

advisors. A great way to find a qualified individual and find out their compensation method is at www.letsmakeaplan.org

2) **Why did You get into the Business?** It's a casual question to get to know the person without being too intrusive, and it will also give insight on what really drives them to help you. What life event motivated them to help others with their finances? Maybe they are in it because they didn't know what they wanted to do after college and went to work for Pops (not a deal breaker, but a flag). Getting to know the passion behind pursuing financial planning as a career will help you understand if they are in it for the long haul and if they truly take an interest in making sure you progress towards your financial objectives. Do they also volunteer or provide pro-bono financial advising to the under-privileged? This is a good sign that they are passionate about their work and want to do what they can to use their skills for the benefit of their community.

3) **How do You come up with the Advice You Give Me?** You should know what resources the planner uses to develop financial or investment recommendations. Do they read financial journals, use

online screeners or Morningstar? Or do they just use some online calculator for asset allocation and throw in some generic index funds you could have done yourself? You want to make sure if you are paying them, that they are adding value to what you are trying to accomplish, such as saving you time or providing their expertise. The other thing is, never invest in something you don't understand, especially when promised with high returns and low risk. If it sounds too good to be true, it probably is.

4) **How will I Know you have my Best Interests in Mind?** One way to do this without asking the question is by looking up their credentials. If they are a CFP, they are held to a fiduciary standard as part of their certification, or plainly as having your best interests in mind when making recommendations. Checkout BrokerCheck on *finra.org*. Certifications also display their commitment to the profession and in continuing education, so they know what they are talking about. Ask if they receive any kick-backs for referring you to a banker, CPA or attorney. Do they look out for load funds so the money you invest actually goes into the investment and not their pocket? Search for the professional you are considering on Google. Also,

check out Investor.gov for links to vetting the background of the planner, such as years in business and if they have any disciplinary actions on file.

5) **What will Happen to Us if You Leave the Business?** As with anything in life, nothing is for certain. If you are going to invest your time, trust and money in a financial planner who works independently, you want to know what happens if/when they sell their practice, change industries, pass away, get sued or whatever else could threaten their continuity. Explore their business succession plan, and if they just brush it off or say they'll figure it out, it's probably time to reconsider your relationship. This is especially true if they are much older than you and nearing retirement. Just ask yourself--if their 23-year-old son suddenly took over your money and gave you advice, would you feel just as comfortable? What if this change happened while you were away, hospitalized or going through some significant life event? Protect yourself and know your planner's backup plan.

Five Items to Factor in when Creating an Investment Portfolio

You could read countless articles and read hundreds of books that will tell you how to choose investments and allocate your portfolio. For every argument for a certain kind of investment, there is one against it. What you need to know is that only you can determine what is best for you and equip yourself with impartial knowledge from trusted sources. Ask friends, read online forums, and take these five steps as a foundation for developing your portfolio.

1) **<u>Know your Objective</u>:** When you're selecting investments, you first want to determine what the money is for. Retirement? Buying a house? Starting a business? Or maybe, you make so much money you need somewhere to throw it (*If only, #AmIRight?*). This will help you build out what kind of investments you want. For example, if you're saving up for a house in the next five-to-seven years, maybe you want to look for more secure investments, such as a CD or balanced mutual fund/ETF. If the money is for your newborn's college, stocks are your friend.

2) **<u>Know Your Timeline:</u>** This is important because you want to select investments that align with the amount of time you will need to liquidate your investments, as well as to have time to recover from market volatility. So, for retirement in 30 years, you can invest in instruments which have a low liquidity or high volatility in exchange for higher returns (equities). If the money is for a car in a year or two, you probably want to invest cash equivalents or something you can liquidate easily, such as a short-term CD or money market account that won't fluctuate as much if at all.

3) **<u>Know Your Comfort Level with Risk:</u>** This is key, because no matter what financial experts say you *should* invest in, only you know into what you feel comfortable putting your hard-earned money. There are a number of risk-tolerance questionnaires (RTQs) on the web that can help you get started. They'll ask how you would respond to a certain market event or what you are willing to give up in order to earn. Stocks, ETFs, mutual funds, bond funds, real estate, cash and everything in between are potential contenders for your portfolio mix. You just want to make sure you understand and feel comfortable where you put your money and be able to stick it out through

volatility, political turmoil or anything else that will make you feel as if the world is ending.

4) **Know the Fees Associated with what You Buy:** When you decide to open a brokerage (trading) account or IRA, you'll want to figure out what the account minimum is and fees for trading. Some brokerage companies offer free trades for their proprietary funds and ETFs which may work to your benefit. You also want to make sure you understand what fees are involved in the funds you buy. Some mutual funds have sales charges or loads, and all have expense ratios for ongoing management of the fund. I like ETFs for the reason that they trade like stocks (no loads or sales charges) but have the diversification of a mutual fund. Use a screener to find low expense funds that meet your criteria. You can't control what returns you will earn on your investments, but you can control the fees, so look for low expense ratio funds, no transaction fee funds, and ask your brokerage company for free trades. *NerdWallet.com* has a decent guide on how to select a company to open your investment account: NerdWallet Investing

5) **Decide on Your Investment Philosophy and do Your Research:** Are you completely turned off by logging into your account to trade and rebalance, nonetheless research different investments? You may want to look at a professionally managed portfolio, or maybe even a Robo Advisor to get started. If you want to manage your own account, do you want actively managed funds, or more inclined toward a passive index funds strategy? Most brokerage companies have research tabs where you can find out fundamentals, past performance, analyst ratings and more for various stocks and funds. Do you want to screen out companies that invest in fossil fuels, or those that focus on impact investing? This is possible, as well. *Morningstar.com* can provide a star-rating for the funds, along with globe ratings for sustainability. Along with custom screening, many brokerage companies offer an approved list of strong performers in each category, such as large cap value funds or emerging markets funds.

Five Websites for Solid Money Advice

Sometimes the amount of information out on the web may feel overwhelming, and there's no shortage of advice and opinions. The key is sticking with sources that have a track record and are embraced by financial gurus who you might follow. Having scoped most of the major players, I've listed here the ones I've found to have the most valuable, objective tools and advice.

1) **Investopedia.com:** This website is easy to read and is a great place to start to learn basic financial terminology, such as what an IRA is, the difference between a mutual fund and ETF, what a limit order is or different asset classes. I have found it to be very objective in providing unbiased definitions of financial concepts, as well as examples, and then pivots to another relevant concept you might be interested in.

2) **Mint.com:** Most of you have probably heard of this site. One of the perks of this one is the user-friendly interface and simple layout. It's a great tool to see all your accounts, transactions, debts and investments in one place. Also, you can create

custom budgets, and I like the How has *My Net Worth Changed* graph for a little motivation. It lets you create different categories and will follow your spending to keep you on track, provide you with alerts when you go over budget, as well as send you regular financial summaries.

3) **MSN.com/Money:** I like this one because it brings together relevant articles from around the web, everything from daily stock news to general consensus on the economy to practical tips such as easy ways to save on utilities or 30 things you don't realize you are wasting money on. Even I found out I was wasting money. (Never again, paper towels!)

4) **Bankrate.com:** This is a great comparison site to find the best credit cards, savings interest rate, car insurance, etc. It's also got some great calculators to help you get a better picture of your vacation budget or how much of a mortgage you can afford. Like MSN, it provides some great articles and advice on saving, spending, investing and other ways to be fiscally savvy. Thinking of financing your car or finding out the cost of living in your dream city? Head to *bankrate.com*, and you'll find it easier to answer those questions.

5) **Morningstar.com:** Known for their ubiquitous star-rating system, Morningstar is one of the most trusted comprehensive tools when it comes to evaluating different mutual funds and ETFs, among other instruments. Let's say you're thinking about which of the 47 fund options you should choose for your 401(k). You can type in the symbol and fund names to compare expense ratios, performance, what stocks the funds invest in and more. They do a good job of illustrating risk/reward, and the ratings help you discern whether their analysis shows a fund is worth it or not. Looking for *socially responsible* investments? They now have a sustainability score to accompany the stars with, appropriately, globes. Investments that have strong performance ratings and sustainability ratings = win/win. Plus, check with your local library. You can usually get access to *morningstar.com* through your library card!

Five Financial Accounts You Should Consider Opening

As you may know, there are different types of accounts for different goals. Whether you are saving for your first home, dream vacation, retirement or starting your own wedding planning business, some accounts are better than others. Let's dive in!

1) **Credit Union Checking Account:** Yes, a credit union checking account. Why? Why would I give up the ubiquitous nature of the megabanks? What if I need an ATM? Here is my argument. First of all, credit unions are generally member-owned, so you get better rates on credit cards, loans, savings, etc. You also develop a relationship with the bank people, so if you have an overdraft or need a cashier's check on the fly, they'll take care of you. You'll also be keeping your money more local, so it supports your community instead of being funneled to build some oil well on the other side of the country. Lastly, when was the last time you heard of a credit union taking advantage of its customers by creating fraudulent accounts? Or being on the verge of collapse when they over-leveraged themselves? About the ATMs, I honestly never find

myself going to one. Who uses cash anymore? You can use Venmo or other apps to pay friends back, and most stores will give you cash back when you're already buying your groceries. Still not satisfied? Well, read on, ATM friend.

2) **Online Savings Account:** Ah, see you didn't even have to read that far. One benefit of some online banks is that they provide reimbursement for any ATM fees incurred. Now, there are normally some limitations, such as a $5,000 minimum balance requirement or only up to $15 in fees reimbursed per month. Aspiration Bank, Charles Schwab High Yield Investor Savings and Fidelity Cash Management Account all reimburse ATM fees paired with their own stipulations. Always check the websites as their terms can change. The other reasons you should consider an online savings account--the rates are generally higher, and it also takes longer to withdraw money from the accounts, meaning you'll (hopefully) be less likely to raid your savings when you want to go on a shopping spree. These kinds of accounts work great if you're saving for home in two years or just want to stash six months' worth of living expenses for emergencies.

3) **Roth IRA:** This account is truly a star when it becomes a part of your overall portfolio. Unless you make more than $196,000 in 2017, you can contribute to one. While you can't deduct the contributions like a Traditional IRA, when you're young you probably won't be in the highest tax bracket of your life. Your contributions grow tax free and you can withdraw from the account tax free after you turn 59 ½. You can also take *contributions* out penalty and tax free, given the account has been open for five years, as well as use up to $10,000 towards the purchase of your first home. Always check the tax man's page first for changes: https://www.irs.gov/retirement-plans/roth-iras

4) **Traditional IRA:** Now, you may not contribute the annual maximum to BOTH a Traditional IRA AND a Roth IRA ($6,000 if you're under 50 for 2020 must be the total amount between Roth and Traditional), however, there is a reason for this. More than likely, you're not going to be in the same company at 65 as you were at 25. Therefore, you probably will have retirement plans from each employer. Rather than have nine retirement plans by the time you turn 50, consider opening a Traditional IRA when you leave your employer.

Consolidation will usually make things easier for you to manage and you may have more investment options. There are some advantages to keeping funds in your employer plans, such as creditor protection, so be sure to do your research (on one of the five websites I recommended) before pulling the trigger.

5) **Brokerage Account:** Okay, so you're rolling your eyes at me thinking, "Do you really expect me to have anything left over after all that!?" Well, possibly. If you have built up your savings account to have six months' worth of living expenses and you've also saved for your vacation next year, a brokerage account may be a good idea for you. This is a taxable account where you can invest in stocks, mutual funds, ETF's--basically most types of publicly traded investments. If you have a goal beyond five years, such as starting capital for a business, this is a good way to grow that money. Additionally, if you came into a bonus and want to sock it away for future plans or just want to "play" with the market, this account will let you do that. If you're one of the lucky ones who make more than the IRA thresholds, this account lets you invest as much as you want into the market.

Five Items to Discuss with Your Partner before Tying the Knot

Divorce is expensive, so don't do yourself a disservice by legally entering a marriage without being on the same page, financially speaking. As any experienced financial advisor will tell you, most couples who divorce never get to the same level of financial comfort that they would have been in had they stayed married. I'm not saying to marry someone for money but marry someone who feels the same way you do about it.

1) **Who has Debts:** Look, I get that no one wants to bring up the dark question of debt. However, you are planning to live the rest of your life with this person, combine finances, a home and maybe a family. When you marry, in most cases, their debt becomes your debt. Maybe cook a nice dinner and then sit down, preferably on the same side of the couch, and just be honest. Tell them how much you care about them and that you want to live the rest of your life with them. Honesty is key in a relationship. Are there student loans, car loans, burgeoning credit card bills or erratic spending habits? This will help you both formulate a plan for debt repayment. Be a partner with them, not a

bully. Remember, you are in this together. If they refuse to share this information, take it as a red flag and run the other way. Otherwise, be prepared for a life of arguments and potential financial instability down the road.

2) **Budget Rules:** So, which one of you is the spender? Who makes more or will make more? Does one of you already own the place where the both of you will be living? Don't just assume because your girlfriend spends $500 a month on shoes and manicures, it will justify you spending the same amount on eating out and beer money. If you are going to combine your household, you'll want to divide up who will pay for what. This makes sure you've both got skin in the game and the other person knows you are not going to bail them out if they just overspent and can't afford to pay the internet bill. Respect each other's spending habits and ensure your expenses are being met accordingly at the same time.

3) **Kids and Parents:** Do you want to have kids? How many? Is adoption an option? What about if one of your children is special needs? Having this conversation before starting a family is crucial to prevent an emotional event from creating a financial

nightmare. Kids are not cheap, and if you think you'll see how you feel, and all of a sudden after the second kid your wife wants another, this may create a tumultuous relationship between the both of you. Will one of you stay home to raise them while the other supports the family? Are either of your parents close by and willing to care for them while the both of you work? I'd also recommend asking your partner if they want their parents to live with the both of you when you marry. Extended family living situations are becoming more common now and can sometimes be financially beneficial. Will they contribute to household needs? What about when they are aging? From what resources will you draw to pay for that care?

4) **Priorities for Saving:** Having a conversation around what both of you want out of life and finding some things in common will also help with the budgeting conversation. Are the both of you avid travelers? Maybe agree to set aside $200 per month for your biannual vacation. Do you want to buy a house together? Have a child? Start a business? Does one of you want to go back to school and will need to rely on the other for support? Strategically planning out these milestones in life and

agreeing on what resources you are willing to commit to them will not only start you on the trajectory towards these mutual goals, it will also bring you both closer together, knowing that you are two partners working towards a series of goals you both jointly desire.

5) **Financial Infidelity:** This is most often the result when a conversation around the above topics fails to take place. How did you react when you found out your boyfriend spent $1100 on a guy's night the weekend you were away? Do you think you might react differently when your household and finances are combined? Probably. We don't ever want to get to this step of financial infidelity, as it can create irreparable cracks in the relationship which may ultimately dismantle your marriage. It should come as no surprise that the number one cause of divorce in the United States is financial problems. If you hid something from your girlfriend/boyfriend in the past, being honest now will save you a boatload of stress later on. Have the conversation on anything you have hidden from each other in your dating years. How did that make the other person feel? What consequences can you both agree on, should one of you cheat financially in the future? Hold each other

respectfully accountable and make sure you are on track for the savings goals you have set out for yourself.

Five Unconventional Ways
to Save on Your Wedding

This is a big one. This is the only day you can go all out, the most important day in your life! Exactly. Do you really want to spend a year's salary on a single day? Hopefully, that will be your only wedding. You can have fun, make it an indelible extravaganza, and still have funds left over for a nice vacation, home or just a financial cushion. I won't mention the obvious, such as invite less people, make your own centerpieces and avoid wedding season dates. Hopefully, these tricks will add to your toolkit on nuptial savings.

1) **Avoid Costly Printed Invitations:** I often see my friends mailing fancy *Save The Date* cards, as well! If you text your friends and Instagram your every meal to keep connected to the world, use email for invites. Sites like Evite, Greenvelope and Paperless Post make gorgeous invitations, and your guests can easily archive them in their email, respond on the spot and download the event details to their calendars. You can also manage your guest list, message guests and send reminder RSVPs or updates. Not only is this cheaper, but you're also saving time (ordering, detailing, labeling, etc.),

eliminating stamps, reducing clutter and saving the environment.

2) **Forgot a Full Open Bar:** It's no secret that alcohol is expensive. One of my good friends who worked as a server and then bartender for many years states that food does not make a restaurant money--the alcohol does. If you have a full bar, that's adding whiskey, vodka, hard liquor, etc. where beer, wine and a few custom cocktails will do just fine. Remember how creative you were at college parties when budgets didn't really allow for fancy drinks? You don't have to go that extreme but consider that mindset. Also, ask the bar to provide smaller glasses. The next time you go to a party or wedding, you'll notice many people order a drink, take a few sips, run off to meet someone or take a picture and forget/neglect where they left it. Many drinks go to waste, which is money literally going down the drain (pun intended).

3) **Ask Friends and Family First for Vendors:** Asking friends and family is the best way to start, because they generally will give you candid feedback on using various vendors. Not only can this save you time as opposed to relentlessly searching Google

or wedding magazines, but it may also save you money because the vendor wants repeat business, and some have referral discounts. Maybe Aunt Doris used an amazing local bakery for a cake, knows the owner and can help you get a great deal. Or your cousin Austin used a rookie DJ at a fraction of the cost of a professional, yet everyone still had a blast and enjoyed the music. The other thing you can do is ask the venue if they have referrals and can get you a discounted rate by going in-house. Remember though, always comparison shop!

4) **Check Out Municipal Facilities:** Most cities have community halls, sports/recreation centers, park pavilions and other gathering spaces for use of the residents. A simple Google search for "[Your City] Community Center" can reveal potential locations. Not only might you be eligible for a discounted rate as a tax-paying resident of that city, but because municipalities are not for-profit, their rates are typically very competitive. I've also found that city-owned venues are less strict on what kind of vendors you can use, what decorations you can set up and have more lax requirements on alcohol and reservation times. They probably won't be as glamorous as the Grand Ballroom of the Ritz

Carlton, but will you really notice when you're dancing the night away with everyone you love?

5) **Solicit Businesses to Provide Samples:** This is truly for the savvy personal finance expert, getting companies to give you free stuff in exchange for allowing them to advertise to your wedding guests. You may have to think outside of the box for this one and prepare yourself for plenty of rejections, but who cares, if it's free? Maybe in exchange for placing their business cards at dinner tables, the local bakery will provide free desserts. Or by providing them a slide in your slideshow, the linen rental company will give you all your chair covers for free. I've even heard of a couple who got 150 free stainless-steel water bottles with the couple's initials and date on the front and the company's logo on the back! If you're sensitive about how your guest will perceive this kind of advertising, then maybe go with the more subtle items.

Five Ways to Save Money on Throwing a Party

If you've ever thrown a party, you know there always seems to be things you didn't expect to spend money on, or you spent too much on. But one thing is for sure--you probably spent more than planned. The broken coffee table from jumping off the couch: $500. The video of you doing a backflip in your living room surrounded by all your friends: Priceless. Yes Mastercard, memories are priceless, but if we can save money on partying, it's on!

1) **Throw it at Home:** One of the largest expenses for throwing a party is the space needed. Think about your own situation. Most of your income goes to rent/mortgage, right? Costs can range from $300 or so for reserving the community room in your building to over $10,000 for a ballroom at a downtown luxury hotel. If you can have the party at home or a friend/relative's house, there is nothing cheaper than free! Now, that does not take into cost the wear and tear of 100 people on your carpets and Italian silk futon. So if you're sensitive to others in your home and have nightmares of the movie *Project X*, then this option may not be for you. You may have to cozy up to friends and family

who have big homes or connections to venues. Otherwise, having a party at home can mean more money for other aspects of the party, or just keeping the cost low.

2) **Be Your Own DJ:** With all of the options of YouTube AutoPlay, iTunes and DIY Party Mix sets for home, you may not have the need for a full-fledged DJ. Now, this again goes with the context of your party. Is it a black-tie wedding reception? In that case, having your teenage cousin behind the wheel of a mixer may not reflect so well. If the party is at home, though, you can do just fine with a laptop and some surround sound or Bluetooth speakers. Download (legally) a playlist of songs and stream it all night long. Another aspect to think about for home parties is the proximity and sensitivity of your neighbors. We threw a party in our backyard once and had the police called on us three times! Maybe bring them cookies or invite them to the party beforehand and ease the tension. Think about what is most important to you and the person the party is for. Is it the music? Food? Decor? All of the above?

3) **Shop Around for Catering:** Aside from venue rental, food is often the most expensive aspect of

a party. While decor, rental and DJ costs can be fixed, the more people you invite, the higher the cost of food. (Do you REALLY want to invite your neighbors now?) Make a mock menu of what you are looking for along with your headcount and discuss it with at least three different catering companies or restaurants. Many will throw in extra perks to forgo lowering the price, such as plates and silverware, a staff bartender, buffet decorations, etc. Just because only one company makes tiramisu cheesecake bites doesn't mean it's worth paying $1000 extra for. You can also get a bunch of appetizers from Costco or bring in food trucks! Be creative, and guests will be sure to have a memorable experience.

4) **Borrow from Friends:** Okay, not to sound like a mooch, but what are friends for, right? If you had 50 centerpiece vases in your garage from your dad's retirement party, wouldn't you enthusiastically lend it to a friend? The sharing economy is what it's all about, people. With all the apps these days, you can share your house, car or outdoor equipment, so why not party supplies? Besides, it's wasteful for every single person throwing a party to buy balloon weights, tealight candles and cake pedestals. Need an extra table for the gifts or

swag stage decorations? Call up people who were recently married or threw a party. Chances are they'll be relieved to find a new use for items stagnating in their garages.

5) **Condense Your Beverage Offerings:** Alcohol is another big expense for a party, especially if you have your heart set on serving Cristal and wine straight from Napa, CA. Instead of hiring a bartender to serve trendy mixed drinks, maybe make one or two signature cocktails that reflect the party's theme. If you can, buy your alcohol in bulk from a warehouse like Costco. Beware, some stores/states have policies that do not allow the return of alcohol, so don't over-buy. You can even entice your guests to drink more lemonade or water--what's cheaper than water? Have a couple of clear beverage dispensers and fill them with different produce, such as mint and lime or strawberry and cucumber. If it's a winter party, maybe a hot chocolate or tea station will work to impress your friends.

Five Household Investments
that will Save You Money

Warning: This list is dependent upon you actually using the products on a regular basis. If you're going to get depressed about not visiting your favorite barista and weep as you drink your homemade coffee, don't buy a $300 coffee machine. However, this is a personal finance book. If any of the following apply to you and you actually invest in and use them, you WILL save a good chunk of change over time.

1) **Iron/Ironing Board:** If you're wearing business professional to the office, you're likely paying your dry cleaner a weekly visit, which for me was running up $10-$20 a week. Since I bought an iron, I can knock out pressing five-to-six shirts and a couple pants in 30 minutes, all while watching the evening news. Check the tags for your shirts and pants. It's likely they are machine washable. Avoid purchasing *dry clean only* clothing, at least for those garments you wear on a regular basis. Or better yet, look for *non-iron* shirts when you next go shopping. Many formal clothing brands now offer *travel collection* dress pants and shirts, which not only allow you to wash and dry on your own

but are more lightweight and breathable and stay dry as you go from lunch to meeting to presentation. Still have wrinkles in them after the dryer? Hang them up in the bathroom while you shower or take them out slightly damp and then iron them.

2) **Cast Iron Skillet:** I strongly feel buying one of these made me want to experiment more with cooking. I bought one for about $30, and you can make all kinds of dinners and desserts with just one pan. It goes on the stove top, into the oven and even on the campfire! These things last forever and they distribute the heat evenly, so you don't burn the onions. There are endless opportunities to cook up something, you'll save by not eating out and you'll have numerous chances to impress your friends with your culinary skills. The best part about these is they are so versatile. You pretty much can't break it. It won't peel like those nonstick pans and all you need to clean them is hot water and a brush.

3) **Coffee Machine:** Okay, as I mentioned earlier, this might be a frivolous expense if you're going to relapse after one week and start sleepwalking to the coffee shop in your lobby. However, if you like

your coffee straight up and drink it for its purpose and not dessert, buying a decent coffee maker can help you save time (not waiting in line at the coffee shop), money (duh), and maybe even your health (no, the double chocolate caramel iced coffee with whipped cream is not *just coffee*). Better yet, convince your boss or office manager to get one for the break room and you'll instantly be an office hero. (Here is where negotiation skills become useful.)

4) **Quality Comforter:** Well, if you pay for your own heating and air conditioning, this can make a difference. You don't really outgrow a comforter like you do with your clothes, so investing in a good one can make sure not only that you don't spend more on one again for a long time, but also that you make sure you are warm when you need to be to prevent turning up the heat. Sure, you could dress like an Eskimo with gloves and all to stay warm, but can you really sleep in that? I didn't think so!

5) **Good Shower Head:** Okay, fine, maybe this is a luxury. But I can't tell you how much a good shower can power-start your day. If you have an old, clogged-up shower head that sadly dribbles out

148 · GARY GREWAL

water, you're probably not going to jump out dancing to *Walking on Sunshine*. On the other hand, getting a nice rain shower with a robust flow, or a handheld to make it more "engaging," you'll feel more energized and thus have a more bubbly, productive day (C'mon, I know you've seen those commercials of people getting started with their day. They all have good shower heads!) Bonus, you'll save on your water bill too, not only because newer ones are more efficient, but with a powerful shower you probably won't spend as much time running that water.

Five Items to Rent Instead of Buy

With an economy that is increasingly based on shared assets intangible property and experiences, there is less reason to individually own an item that loses value and that you use intermittently. In the long run, renting or borrowing items can save you money, help your friends and family and be less burdensome.

1) **A Car:** This is especially true if you live in the city or near good public transportation. Next to living expenses, having a car can be next, with a car payment, registration, parking, gas, insurance, and maintenance. Living in a city, I can walk to work, the grocery store, the farmer's market, the gym, running trails, restaurants, and nightlife! I've put about 3,000 miles per year on my car. As I write this, it's on sale. Even if you live in the burbs and use public transportation to get to work, you may want a car to run errands or to go on a day trip. Well, in addition to Uber and Lyft, there are also an increasing number of car-share programs you can use for when you're dreading lugging those groceries back on the bus. Car2Go, ZipCar, Maven and other local programs are all options. Bike sharing programs can help with shorter

distance trips or those between transit stops. Check if they have them in your town. If not, request them.

2) **Recreational Equipment:** Unless you've picked one hobby and do it religiously, it doesn't always make sense to buy a snowboard, kayak, mountain bike, jet ski or ATV. Now I'm not saying you should borrow a tennis racket every week; however, are the big-ticket items just a once-in-a-while thing? Many sporting retailers such as REI rent everything from kayaks to snowboards to tents at very affordable prices. Or try the app Fluid Market. You would have to use your kayak 30 or so times to make up for the price difference in renting, plus the wear and tear, transportation and storage. Or maybe you have a friend with a paddleboard, and you've got a tent. Perfect for swapping! If you haven't noticed, we've become a nation of accumulation. Rent when you can and live a simple life. Pick one or two hobbies, commit to them and then buy the mandatory equipment (preferably used).

3) **Formal Attire:** Now this tip applies more to ladies, but it's for guys, too. I can't believe some dates I had in high school or college. I'd find out some girls paid up to $500 for a dress and then never

wore it again! Thankfully, services such as Rent the Runway have come around since then. People get so sentimental about keeping their wedding outfits or their first homecoming dress, and then it's shoved in the back of a closet for 30 years. For guys, renting or borrowing may be in your favor. If you don't wear a suit to work, you probably don't need more than one suit, a couple of dress shirts and ties and one pair of dress shoes. Having an older brother, I borrowed clothes and even his graduation gown!

4) **Specialty Tools:** Bought your first place? Want to finally tackle that bathroom remodel? Don't go on a shopping spree to the hardware store just yet. First, take an inventory of what you have and then what you need. Which inexpensive items can you buy, such as a paint brush, versus rent or borrow, such as a table saw? You may be surprised to know that retailers like Lowe's and The Home Depot rent tools such as air sprayers, chainsaws and generators. Want to save even more money? Ask your neighbors! Make sure to offer your own tools in return or to help them on any upcoming projects they have. If it's been a one-way street for too long, hand them a gift or invite them over for dinner. If you're really ambitious, start a

neighborhood tool library. Put a shed together, and everyone can contribute seldom-used items. Go off the honor system and sign in, use a camera or have some of the neighborhood kids volunteer to man the shed.

5) **Electronic Gadgets:** Let's say you're having a pool party or movie night and your sound system is lame. Are you really going to shell out $800 for a premium center bar speaker or surround sound system? I wouldn't recommend secondhand here, as you never know what condition they are in, and usually secondhand sales will void any warranty. Whether you need a projector, flood lights, a camera or string lights, there are many items you can simply rent or borrow. Check your local retailers such as Rent-A-Center, or even the library, to see what items they have for rent. It's also likely that your friends have some of the stuff you'll need for your party or project. The same courtesy applies here, to return the favor or thank them in some way for letting you use their stuff. The MOOCH app is an option here, as well.

Five Things You Need to Stop Buying to Save Your Money

Do you loathe garbage day or grind your teeth when you take the trash out? Where does all this stuff come from? It's literally throwing your money away. There is no shortage of advertisements everywhere you look, from bus benches to TV, luring us to buy stuff we don't really need but are made to believe we do. Don't get caught up in the mindless culture of consumption. Cut these things out and save your cash.

1) **Bottled Water:** Okay, honestly, this one gets me big time. Not just because people waste money on something they can get for free, but also the waste it generates. These bottles are ubiquitous in the worst places possible: parks, beaches, hiking trails, lakes, you name it. In any case, you can get a stainless-steel water bottle for less than $10, and anywhere you go, you can fill it up for free. You can even score one of them for free at a job fair, convention or festival. If you still need convincing, go watch the documentary *Tapped*. Save money, save the planet.

2) **Paper Towels:** I stopped using these a few years ago when I realized I can get a pack of cotton cloths for less than $5 at Target. Guess what? I still have them, and they work great. Just pop them in the washing machine once a week and use the sanitize cycle or wash them in hot water. Pretty sure ONE pack of paper towels costs more than $5 and lasts maybe a week or two. Think about what you use paper towels for. Normally it's cleaning or wiping up a spill. Sponges and cloth towels work great for that! Plus, they are way more absorbent than a paper towel. Don't want to buy them? Tear up some old T-Shirts or towels. You'll also clog up your trash less and be green.

3) **Disposable Cleaning Wipes:** Sure, they might be convenient, and you love that weird pseudo-lemon smell. However, you probably realize that you go through them pretty quick. It's just another one of those things where you're paying for convenience. Instead, just buy a biodegradable all-purpose cleaner (My favorite is *Method*. They have pleasant scents like Lavender and Clementine for $2.99) and then use your cleaning cloths! It'll last you much longer. You can even make your own cleaner with baking soda and other household

items, but I don't want to push you so far that it totally backfires, and you hire a cleaning service.

4) **Single-Use Mop Inserts:** Okay, Swiffer fans, here is a downer for you. I know those catchy commercials make it seem so easy. Just slip a refill cloth on, mop and throw it away! What they don't tell you is you're throwing money away, too! Get yourself a floor mop with a microfiber cloth (around $15). I have one and the cloth is really powerful. Just splash it with some hot water, a couple sprays of all-purpose cleaner, and voila! Then just pop it in the washer along with your cloth cleaning towels (see that selfish plug?) and you'll never have to worry about running out of mop refills. Plus, save money and waste!

5) **Plastic Sandwich Bags:** Yes, this hits the convenience factor once again. Just work with me for a second. How many things do you use resealable plastic bags for? Most of the uses, such as for a sandwich, berries, nuts or a leftover avocado, can be accomplished by using glass or durable-plastic containers. These containers are also better, as they are usually spill proof, airtight and prevent your beloved swiss and turkey sandwich with

honey Dijon from getting soggy. Plus, have you ever had your berries squished when you opened up your lunch? Yeah, that's fun. Save money, save on waste and save your lunch.

Five Questions to Ask Yourself before Making a Purchase

Unless you've been living under a rock, I'm sure you've heard of the phrase, *Keeping Up with the Joneses*. From mindless impulse purchases to shelling out for luxury goods we can't afford or don't really need, asking yourself a few questions can help you form the habits of a more conscious consumer.

1) **Do I Really Need This?** I know this seems obvious, but you'd be surprised how many people just casually shop, both in stores and online. Have you ever dropped by Target to pick up a few toiletries and ended up spending $60? If you just get into the habit of picking up something and asking if you need it, you'll be surprised at how that brief pause can help you save your wallet. Emotions can be a powerful thing. We have a bad day at work and *deserve* a new pair of shoes. We convince ourselves we need new $300 headphones because the old ones are out of fashion. I'm not saying you should ask yourself if you really need something for every item at the grocery store (it's okay to splurge on food once in a while), just open your wallet *mindfully*, not *mindlessly*.

2) **What Value does this Bring into My Life?** We don't always buy things we need, per se; however, some just bring us contentment. A new jacket for work, a new laptop for your side gig or a gourmet blender for your hobby of baking or making drinks, for example. You should buy things that bring you genuine happiness, things you consciously feel enhance your lifestyle. I have a friend who loves cars and drives a $40,000 Audi, but meal preps for the week. A colleague of mine loves designer bags but drives a 2007 Nissan Sentra. When you buy things you like, ask yourself what value this will bring into your life. How many kitchen appliances do I really use? I don't cook that often! Will I really enjoy spending $800 to upgrade my phone just because my friends have new ones, or am I fine with this one?

3) **If I don't have this Now, will I be any Less Happy?** Even if something does bring you value or happiness, how might you feel a week, a month or a season from now if you don't have it? Or maybe you'll feel better when you buy it once other priorities, such as paying off debt, are taken care of. Sure, it may feel cool to drop $1000 on a new snowboard, but if you go to the slope three times

and then the season is over, is the board really going to enhance your memories of the season? If you don't buy that new Smart TV, are you going to think about it every day for the next week? Are you going to keep using a massage chair, or will you find greater joy getting a real massage done once in a while? Try to think forward in your life. You didn't have this specific item before, so if you don't have it, ask yourself if it will genuinely alter your satisfaction with your life in the future. It's kind of like that new car effect. A new purchase is exciting for maybe the first month, and then you get used to it and fall back to your normal level of satisfaction. Don't fall into the consumerism trap, shopping just to shop!

4) **What might I have to Give Up for This?** Unless you're a trustafarian or heir to some fortune, you probably can't buy everything your heart desires. So the next time you want to make an impulse purchase on Amazon or while window shopping, ask yourself, "If I spend this now, is it going to prevent me from doing anything else I want to do this month? Am I okay with that?" This will help bring to the front of your mind other expenditures you may have. Perhaps you're going on a destination wedding next month or a vacation to Europe. If

you buy some gadget or accessory you don't really need or want, maybe you'll have less funds for buying a souvenir, enjoying a nice dinner or buying better tickets to a concert you've been longing to see. And don't even think about saying "Oh I'll just put in on my card and pay it off next month, YOLO!" You now know better than that!

5) **Is there Another Time/Way I can get This Cheaper?** Now, if you really have your heart set on spending for a certain item or service, the next best thing you can do is see if you can obtain it at a cheaper price. If you want a new snowboard, wait until Spring when outdoor retailers put them on clearance to make way for new inventory. New chaise? Ask if the floor model is for sale for a discount or ask the manager what happens to returned items. Online is even easier. Just do a simple Google search or use one of the many *price-watch* apps such as *SlickDeals*. You can also search for coupon codes and promo codes, and make sure you read up on the company's price-match policy. This applies to services, as well. Ask your masseuse or caterer if they'll beat other prices or take discounts.

Five Books to Read that will Save/Earn You Money

Being such a devoted fan of libraries, of course I am also an even bigger fan of books, particularly nonfiction. Going at your own pace to learn about different concepts that interest you (such as personal finance!) is such a productive self-improvement exercise. I wish I could list all the books I love, but here are the top five I suggest you put on your list.

1) ***The Automatic Millionaire* by David Bach:** This book was one of the biggest eye-openers for me, forcing me to look at the big picture. Think you're doing a good job by bringing your lunch to work every day and then binging on a $200 five-course dinner on the weekend? Yeah, sometimes budgeting can only go so far in helping you save more for long-term goals. Enter my biggest takeaway from this book: *Pay yourself first.* What this means is to set up automatic contributions to your retirement plan, your investment account and your savings account. That way, you can only spend what is left and become accustomed to living off the portion of your income dedicated to spending. Another tip from this book is to set up your bills to be paid

automatically so you never incur late fees or risk damaging your credit.

2) ***The Millionaire Next Door* by Thomas J. Stanley and William D. Danko:** So, you think that friend of yours who drives a Porsche and lives in an upscale high-rise condo is rolling in the dough, huh? Think again. He probably is racking up debt just to support his image and cushy lifestyle. This book will really open your eyes to who is actually a millionaire on the books. They don't drive fancy cars, live in gated community mansions or buy top-of-the-line fashion. If you want to emulate behaviors of the genuine wealthy, read up on this book. It may just change your outlook on spending in lieu of achieving long-term financial success.

3) ***The Wall Street Journal Guide to Understanding Personal Finance* by Kenneth Morris and Virginia Morris:** This book provides clear objectives to cross off your list over and above the general guidance of saving and investing (which is just as important). It has useful tips for commonly overlooked items such as scoping out your employer's HR website for free services (consultation with a credit counselor, a financial advisor or a family therapist) as well as discounts (for athletic clubs,

tax services, renting an apartment, transit, etc.). It also has tips such as always having $20 in your wallet to avoid credit card or ATM fees in a situation or taking a picture of items you have for insurance purposes in cash they are stolen, damaged or destroyed.

4) **_Happy Money_ by Elizabeth Dunn and Michael Norton:** Probably the biggest reason I love this book, and think you will too, is that it doesn't just provide mundane methods for saving money or earning more. It discusses proven ways the money makes us HAPPY. Isn't that the end goal in life? I have to say once I adopted some of the methods in this book such as _Buy Time_ and _Give Back_, it substantially dissipated most of my frivolous spending habits. I cared more about creating experiences with friends rather than buying a home entertainment system. Spending in ways that truly have a positive impact on your happiness and outlook on life will naturally help you save money because you don't find yourself binging on a shopping spree or new gadgets just to fill a void. You're happy with things that matter in life and you have what you need.

5) *Save BIG* **by Elizabeth Leamy:** This book provided many ideas on saving money in the context of large purchases such as housing. Large purchases are where it counts most! Some of her tips include after making a down payment, keep saving the amount you were setting aside for a home improvement/maintenance fund or for property taxes. I also like her tips on negotiating realtor commissions, closing costs and fighting junk fees when getting GFE's (Good Faith Estimates). Lastly, her bidding strategy is genius when receiving a counteroffer on a home you're trying to buy--raise your bid *by less than the difference* of what the seller lowered theirs. For example, if the home is listed at $400,000, and you offer $370,000, then they counter with $390,000, you would counter with $375,000.

6) **BONUS!!** I love books so much I'm going to give an exclusive extra, ***Your Money or Your Life*** by Vicki Robin and Joe Dominguez. Just a fantastic overall read. This book is the epitome of the message I preach. Read it, take notes and follow the mantra!

Five Low Cost/Free Activities to do with Others (or Solo!)

I know with all the talk out there about spending on experiences versus material possession", you're thinking, "What CAN I spend my money on--nothing??" Let's be honest, though. Who has trouble finding ways to spend? If you can have a memorable experience by spending less or nothing while also making an impact or improving your sense of gratitude, why not?

1) **Volunteer:** This one is truly one of my favorites. You get to attend an event for free, meet new people and be hands-on in an area that interests you. Triple win! Volunteering can help you gain new skills, meet new friends, improve your social understanding, and take the focus off your own troubles. You can do anything from volunteering at the local film festival, being a volunteer with Boys and Girls Club, building trails with your local land trust or using your professional skills pro bono for those in need. Any way you choose, you're helping to be a pillar in your community and can feel good in that you're making the world a better place. Not only that, I have seen firsthand how previously tense relationships can grow

stronger and more resilient, as you're not focusing on your relationship, but rather connecting through an altruistic activity.

2) **Hiking:** When was the last time you regretted going hiking? Okay, except for the time you were trying to take a selfie with the waterfall and ending up falling down the hillside (just one more reason to shun selfies!). Research has proven that being in nature revitalizes and calms us, brings us back our soul and the feeling of being human. Don't just take my word for it. Read ***The Nature Fix*** by Florence Williams. Take some friends or your parents with you and you'll all enjoy the sunshine, a nice breeze, exceptional views, laughter, oh--and exercise! To find nearby trails, just search *trailhead* in Google maps or search on www.alltrails.com (or the app). While most trails are free, there may be a fee to park or to enter a National Park, so be sure to carpool or bike in. If it's free all around and you enjoy certain spots often, think about donating or volunteering for the group that cares for your trails.

3) **Picnic in the Park:** Oh, here we are, nature once again! This one is a good way to spend time with grandma or the cousin who recently twisted his

ankle and can't hike. Pack some sandwiches (or make them there), fruit, nuts, cookies, or whatever you fancy and take a blanket, maybe some reading material, music and voila! Find a nice spot under some trees or by the creek and you're set for an afternoon of relaxation, volleyball, good eats, and intimate, leisurely conversations about life. In a society consumed by digital communication, few opportunities remain to simply talk to those you love while being surrounded by nature. A picnic does just that. Oh, and it's free, reduces stress, and calms you!

4) **Bike Ride:** Remember the days of childhood, biking around the neighborhood with your friends to get ice cream or hang out at the cool house down the street? This one is one of my close second favorites. If you live by bike trails, consider yourself blessed. Going for a bike ride is another way to get some exercise, fresh air and sun with the family or your buddies. I bike everywhere as long as I don't have to ride back in the dark or in bad weather. This activity is fun as well, because your terrain and landscape is constantly changing, so it keeps things interesting. Don't have friends or family into biking? Go solo for some self-reflection and peaceful *me time*. Or join a cycling club. To

convince your friends to go with you, remind them that bikes don't take gas, don't cost money to register, park or get their oil changed. Bike while you can, before your health turns on you.

5) **Game Night:** Okay, so maybe you're not an outdoorsy person or the weather outside isn't so great. Game night! Regular board games work, and nowadays I've seen many games being played on smartphones. (Can anyone guess that game where a person holds a phone on his forehead, and everyone screams clues to the answer on the screen?) Game night is fun because it also allows for casual conversations, jokes, camaraderie, intimate conversation, and excitement. You should see your Aunt Meredith cheer when she wins at chess--I mean who knew she had so many sarcastic jokes up her sleeve? Don't have any? Here is where the handy dandy library comes in. Ask a friend to bring a game or play good old charades. It's a great way to bring the family together weeknight evenings or to talk to your roommate about things other than cleaning the dishes.

Five Ways to Cheer Yourself Up, other than Impulse Shopping

Let's face it--we all have bad days and try to find ways to get out of the blues. Sometimes, larger life events such as the demise of a relationship can be pretty traumatic, so we try to take our mind off it by eating/drinking/shopping our way out of it. Again, you should always treat yourself with conscious spending up to a limit. However, when we are filled with emotions, we may book that trip to Mexico because we convince ourselves we need to get away without thinking of the consequences to our bottom line when we get home. The last post has some ideas, though the following ideas are more geared towards this specific purpose and are also free or relatively cheap.

1) **Take the Focus off Yourself:** The more we dwell on our personal problems, the longer it will take us to kick our rumination habits. You can let your creativity soar here. Offer to run errands for an elderly neighbor or mow their lawn. Give your great uncle a call if you haven't spoken in a while--it will surely make him feel over the moon. Maybe even consider tutoring struggling school kids or serving on a crisis hotline. Bring treats to relief workers or patients in a hospital. Read a global magazine or

newspaper about people around the world facing much more dire circumstances. Try anything that will shift your focus onto things bigger than yourself and help you create a sense of, "I'll get through this. Compared to others I'm doing pretty good."

2) **Listen to Music:** Have you ever listened to your favorite beats and not felt immensely better? Imagine how boring life would be without music. It brings us together, helps us express ourselves and makes our body move in a way that brings ecstatic, unrestrained joy. (Well, not if you're listening to sad songs. Don't do that if you're trying to feel happy.) You can do this lying on your bed and then dance as if nobody's watching (hopefully no one other than your pet) or go to a music festival, outdoor concert or anywhere you're comfortable going on your own and immersing yourself in the moment.

3) **Keep a Gratitude Journal:** I was the biggest skeptic about this until I tried to commit to it for at least a month. It may not be the first thing you think of when you're down in the dumps, but it will gradually help you see the silver lining in things just when it feels as if everything is going wrong. Many

therapists and self-help gurus testify to the bene-fits of gratitude and mindfulness to increase your satisfaction and in life and bolster your resilience. One thing I started doing was writing about three things that went well that day, week or weekend. Another thing you can try when things are rough is write down three, five or 10 things for which you are grateful. Good health, a roof over your head, loving parents, a promising career, or something as simple as recognizing someone holding the door open for you or the driver who gave you space to merge when you almost missed your exit.

4) **Sweat it Out:** Ah, here it is again! Before you roll your eyes, know that it doesn't have to be an hour-long jog on a treadmill followed by squats. It can be whatever you find interested at that moment and for however long you want. Run on a trail and say hi to everyone who crosses your path (or listen to music, whatever fits your mood). Go for a casual swim or a bike ride. Join a karaoke spin class, vinyasa yoga, beat the crap out of a punching bag or a cardio kickboxing class. You don't have to go to a gym or pay for these. Many classes can be found via subscription programs or even YouTube.

5) **Watch Comedy:** Another beauty of life is that of unrestrained laughter. Do you remember the last time you laughed so hard your stomach hurt? How did you feel afterward? Pretty darned elated, I would hope. Again, you don't have to physically go to a comedy show (though many bars have standup open-mic nights with no cover). You can rent a comedy movie from the library, watch Saturday Night Live skits on YouTube, or find solace in those America's Funniest Home Videos reruns. Maybe even go through your college albums and laugh at the stupid things you did or watch the videos you recorded for birthdays, trips and other things that will bring a smile to your face. All it takes is a little laughter and self-forgiveness to dust ourselves off and charge back into our lives!

Five Ways to Save on Ski Season

The reason this gets its own section is because I didn't realize how many people are into skiing or snowboarding and how much it costs. Equipment, passes, gas, parking, tune ups, you name it. If you're going to jump into this hobby, heed these tips below to validate your involvement and stay on track with your other money goals.

1) **Buy a Season Pass:** This one is pretty clear if you see yourself going more than a half a dozen times. At least in Colorado, a typical day pass can run over $150 each. If you buy a yearly pass and snow sports are one of your *conscious spending* pursuits, make sure to use it. Don't be one of those people who gets all excited when you buy a gym membership and never goes after the first two weeks. Decide what hobbies to which you are going to commit and then embrace them! Money is meant to allow you freedom to pursue your passions, as well. The other thing to consider is many employers provide fitness reimbursements which may include a season pass for skiing/snowboarding. Typically, they will not provide reimbursement for just one day pass but check with your employer.

2) **Sign Up for Ski Resorts' Email Lists/FB:** Sound familiar? These days, with so much competition, ski resorts are looking for attention on social media. Maybe they'll have a flash sale on a Thursday morning for 50% off for the first 100 people who like their post or something similar. Email is a great option, as well, as they might try to fill up some slow days by offering a *Parched March* deal or anniversary sale to celebrate 20 years in business. Again, how often you check or how many lists for which you sign up depends on how often you plan to visit during the winter. If you're prowling the sites weekly before you head out on the weekend, maybe buy a pass.

3) **Check for Coupons/Discounts at Local Sporting Retailers:** Remember when you used to get $15 off a Six Flags ticket by buying a case of soda or how your local gas station sold State Fair tickets at a discount? Similar thinking here. Ski shops, sporting stores, even grocery stores and Costco may have discounted lift tickets, or a buy three get one free, $50 food credit at the resort, etc. This might especially pay if you are just going with a group or your family for the weekend. The other thing to consider is asking the ski resort if they offer

student/senior/military/first responders/educators discounts.

4) **Check with Membership Programs or Online Deals:** First, try online. You'd be surprised at how many deals you can find from a simple Google search. Maybe when you are browsing *Trip Advisor* for ski resorts, an ad shows up that fits your needs. Or you find a Groupon deal, coupon code or even a Meetup that is going and trying to get a group rate. You might also check out *Liftopia.com*, which is kind of like *Expedia.com* for ski resorts. As for membership programs, I'm referring to *AAA*, your professional career association, alumni membership or corporate discounts through your HR. I've even gotten discounts on attractions and theme parks through my local credit union!

5) **Avoid Trendy Resorts, Holiday Weekends:** Now, for the somewhat obvious tips. Yes, you are probably going to pay more on weekends, as that is when most people visit. However, there is no need to spend your Thanksgiving or Christmas at a crowded ski resort and pay through the nose just to have to wait for a lift for 45 minutes each time you want to go up a run. Prices also seem to decline after the holidays and especially as Spring

approaches and the viability of snow is dubious. Also, the most popular (and expensive) resorts will probably show up first during a search or your friend's Facebook feed, and so what? Do your homework, ask the locals, and you can probably find resorts that are closer and less crowded, as well as lower prices for food, parking and lift tickets, to a point. Remember, you're not just buying a lift ticket. You usually have to pay to park, you'll need to eat, and you'll possibly need accommodations if you're staying the weekend. All of those are opportunities to save money!

Five Ways to Save Money on Shopping for Clothes

Yes, I did say one way to invest in yourself is buying good quality clothing items. So, the first tip is to not buy superfluous clothing but quality staples. And since those are usually more expensive than buying tank tops at Target, here are some ways to save on them so you can actually *shop and save*, unlike those commercials that show people maxing out their credit cards while carrying 12 bags after peer-pressure shopping.

1) **Shop Off-Season:** This one is kind of obvious, but I know how some of you just have to have the new board shorts that came out before anyone else or the new versions of suede shoes. However, if saving money is your objective, go for summer clothes around Labor Day or Halloween and winter clothes when the flowers start blooming. I mean, who doesn't feel good when you buy a $300 down jacket for $89 by waiting five months? Now that's delayed gratification.

2) **Use Your Smartphone to Comparison Shop on the Spot:** This should also be easy for all you social-media butterflies. Pretty much everyone has a

smartphone with data these days, unless it's your Uncle Walter in his Montana ranch who would rather mail you a letter every time you text him. With the Internet at your fingertips, you can simply enter the name of the product on Google and use the shopping feature to see what the price is elsewhere. For example, I saw a pair of Kenneth Cole blue suede shoes I wanted at Dillard's and looked up the product number to find it $30 cheaper...on the Dillard's website! Then at Macy's, I bought a carry-on suitcase for $100 less and a dress shirt for $20 less, all by finding it on competitor websites which they happily matched (most of the time). Now, there are also a slew of apps that can search for a cheaper price or even alert you if the price drops within a certain time frame, in case you want to go back to the store for a refund. For me, though, I don't want 128 apps on my phone, so I just search on the spot. If you're an app maniac, here are some suggestions: http://www.digital-trends.com/mobile/best-shopping-apps-iphone-ipad-android/

3) **Go for Machine Washable:** This one is for formal/dress clothes. Do you know how much you're spending on dry cleaning? If you wear a dress or suit to work, the cost for regular dry cleaning can

add up rather quickly. Machine washable dress shirts, for example, are also often non-iron. (I've found this only holds true if you take it out of the dryer as soon as it stops.) The nice thing is, if you actually want to dry clean your machine washable formal clothes, you usually can. However, if they are fine fabrics indicate hand wash or dry clean only, it can cost you a pretty penny to look that posh. For example, I usually buy dress shirts for around $20, and if I dry clean it, it's about $2 a pop. That means after 10 weeks of going to the dry cleaners, I could have just bought a new shirt with that money. And that's not even including the time it takes to drop off/pick up. (I mean, time is money, honey.) Most of my dress shirts and pants I bought three or four years ago are still looking fresh and I've probably dry cleaned them less than five times for special events. Now that's some serious savings.

4) **Sign Up for Loyalty Programs:** Whether it's Macy's, REI or Express, signing up for a loyalty program is easy. If you shop there frequently, why not get rewarded? Loyalty programs shouldn't cost you anything, and generally you can have other special benefits as well, such as extended sale hours or extra time to exchange/return. At REI, I

can be a member for just $20, which pays for itself if I get a bike tune up and some gloves. Plus, you get invited to their amazing *garage sales*, they keep your receipts on file and you get a dividend! How nice it is to save more on clothes by doing pretty much nothing extra. Express will send you coupons such as $20 off your purchase of $75 or more, and Macy's has a cool little savings pass that sometimes will add onto any other savings currently being promoted. These offers always change, so make sure your favorite stores are still keeping good on them.

5) **Don't Dismiss the Clearance Rack or Sale Items:** I get it. Who wants to be that person seen in the corner with all the clothes jumbled together and thrown on the floor? It's like being that one person sorting through the markdown shelf at the grocery store. (Hey, I've done it!) Here is the thing-- while you might think those clothes are on the clearance rack because they are hideous and no one wants them, look at the other side of the coin. Maybe you just happen to be shopping when they just got in their new fall collection for formal attire or jeans and the previous seasons' are on that rack to get rid of. Retailers want to make room for what's hot, and if some of the other stuff doesn't

sell in time, the clearance rack is usually its fate. You've just got to ask yourself, "Do I have the patience to sort through a disorganized rack to find that one steal of a deal?"

Five Protective Financial Measures to Take when You're Young

Ah, youth. The carefree days of life. The days of hanging out with your friends all the time and having the energy to party all night only to show up for class like a boss the next day. Sadly, time is one thing we don't get back, so be sure to also take advantage of youth and good health when you begin to think about your future.

1) **Get Health Insurance:** This is one of the most important types of insurance. One accident or unfavorable diagnosis can destroy your financial situation or prevent you from reaching other financial goals. Most workplaces offer this, although you might have to pay for some of the premium. I personally like the high-deductible type plans. Not only are the monthly premiums cheaper, your employer will usually put money into an HSA (Health Savings Account) which you can use for co-pays toward reaching your deductible. If your employer does not offer health insurance or you are self-employed, you'll have to get it on your own. Try checking if some of the associations or groups you are a part of offer group rates (e.g. National Association of Water Balloon

Enthusiasts). You can also check out this helpful article at *NerdWallet* to shop around: https://www.nerdwallet.com/blog/health/health-insurance-guide/?trk=nw_gn_4.0

2) **Sign Up for Disability Insurance:** Usually, your employer will provide some kind of short-term and long-term disability. Check your benefits to see what is provided. Is it 60% of your base pay? For how long? Look at your spending and see if your essentials can be covered by 60% of your pay. The last thing you want on top of dealing with some kind of disability, is for your finances to be strained due to the lack of income. If you can afford supplemental disability insurance, it may be a good idea, especially if your income (and spending) are going to grow throughout your career. Having an emergency savings fund can help get through the waiting period before benefits start. The longer it is before the benefits start kicking in generally lowers your premiums.

3) **Get a Will and Healthcare Directive:** Don't scoff at this just because you are single with no kids! Chances are, the longer you work, you are going to accumulate things such as bank accounts, a car, a house, a vintage grandfather clock collection,

etc. Rather than leave your affairs in shambles, it is good to be prepared with a will, which you can create on your own (be sure to follow your state's rules regarding this). If you want to give your assets to your parents, sibling or favorite charity, a will can accomplish this and prevent an already traumatic event for your family from being even more unbearable. A healthcare directive ensures that if you are unable to make medical decisions for yourself, you legally appoint someone to do this for you and lay out your wishes (such as resuscitation). Don't make it into a vicious legal battle for your family members. Take care of this while you are young and have healthy cognition.

4) **Verify all Your Accounts have Beneficiaries Listed:** This is one of the easiest things you can do to protect your loved ones or favorite nonprofits. For your retirement accounts, you must list a beneficiary, or it will most likely default to your estate, which kind of defeats the purpose, because those assets now go through probate. You can use *mint.com* to check off each of your listed accounts, and then login to that specific site to ensure your beneficiary information is up to date. Most institutions allow you to do this online. Otherwise, download a form or call the service line. For bank

accounts and stock brokerage accounts, they should let you complete a TOD (Transfer on Death form) or POD (Payable on Death).

5) **Consider Life Insurance:** Life insurance is probably the furthest from your mind right now. I mean what sounds more fun--*I can spend $100 a month on takeout and Netflix* or *I can spend $100 per month on life insurance*...said no one ever. Here is why you should consider it, even if you have no dependents. When you are young and healthy, your cost of insurance is the lowest it will ever be, meaning your premiums will be lower. If you lock in a rate then, it can prevent you from getting a crazy expensive rate or even be declined in the future due to health issues. When you do have a family, you can be sure they are covered because you got coverage when you were young and healthy and can afford to pay it. Plus, if you get term insurance (cheapest) and want to convert it to permanent insurance, you can usually do it without the need for a medical exam.

Five Adult Conversations to have with Your Parents/Siblings

Okay, this is the not-so-fun part. However, not every aspect of life is lollipops and puppies. Having these serious conversations now can not only save you thousands of dollars in the future, it can also prevent strained relationships with your loved ones when the unknowns of life happen. Disclaimer: always consult an attorney for legal advice!

1) **Who is Making Healthcare Decisions for Mom and Dad?** First of all, you'll want to make sure your parents have a Health Care Directive. This is a legal document which allows a person to name an "agent" to make health-care decisions on your behalf or to communicate your wishes to receive treatment if you are not able to do so yourself. Without this document, and conversation around how decisions will be made, there can be tempestuous arguments amongst your family members. Talk to your parents about their wishes, have them create a health care directive and bring in any other relevant family members to ensure they understand the wishes of Mom and Dad while they are of sound mind.

2) **Where are All the Important Documents on Accounts/Family Advisors?** If your parents have assets such as retirement accounts or a business, encourage them to draft a document or spreadsheet that lists what different accounts they have, where they are held and what the login/account information is. Then, I would even have them list each other as "authorized parties" if allowed by the institution where individual accounts are held. This allows the other spouse to access information and perhaps make changes. If your parents also work with financial planners, accountants, etc., ask to tag along on the next meeting so you are familiar with them, how to contact them and provide your parents with an extra set of eyes on how well they are being taken care of.

3) **Who will Manage the Investments and Finances in an Emergency?** If you followed the advice in the last bullet point and had your parents list an authorized party for their accounts, you're headed in the right direction. Now, another family conversation needs to occur on who will make financial decisions if both of them are unable. Perhaps your father deals with the finances and your mother is uncomfortable assuming the responsibilities

alone. If something happens to him, she is going to need help, and you'd rather have this talk now, than when crisis strikes. What if your sister wants a piece of the action? Or your older brother who is a yoga instructor has no desire to deal with finances. These conversations can not only prevent a disastrous unraveling of the family finances, it can also stop relationships from fraying or becoming toxic.

4) **What is the Plan to Take Care of Mom and Dad when They are too Old?** This is a tough one, as talking about one's senility is about as attractive as hearing your loved ones argue about who gets what after your death. No one wants to be dependent on others toward the end of life, but it can happen to even the healthiest people. According to the US Department of Health and Human Services, nearly 70% of people turning age 65 will need long-term care at some point in their lives. I can't tell you how many people just inherently assume their kids will figure it out and take care of them, yet these conversations never happen. When push comes to shove and you have your own family/career to deal with, how will you feel if the responsibility of caring for your parents is suddenly delegated to you? If you have siblings who

live closer to your parents than you, perhaps discuss how if they are the primary physical caretakers, can you and other siblings pitch in financially or deal with other duties, such as financial matters and estate distribution? Talk it out and then hug it out.

5) **Who is Going to Manage the Legal Affairs/Estate when the Parents Pass?** Yet another set of legal documents are called for here. If your parents already created a will or trust, be sure everyone is on the same page as who was named as successor trustee and executor and the reasoning behind it. Discuss with your siblings their comfort level with various responsibilities and make sure it's relatively equal to prevent bad blood in the future. If your parents have not done this kind of planning yet, go with them to meet with an estate planning attorney. Then share the details with the rest of your family. When everyone is in the know about who is getting what and who is going to deal with the distribution of the parents estate and funeral arrangements, the less likely you and the surviving family members will be at each other's throats had your parents passed intestate.

Five Items to Keep in Safe Place
to Protect Your Finances

Don't worry, I'm not going to tell you to go out and buy a bulletproof safe. It is imperative, however, that you keep certain documents in a secure place, because there will be a day you may need one of them. They should never be thrown in a junk drawer, glove box, or jumbled with a bunch of tax returns and albums in your coat closet. Save time and your sanity and get these things in order!

1) **Estate Planning Documents:** As you should know by now, a Living Will is a must-have for all your non-beneficiary designated or pass-by-title property. Make sure someone you know and trust, maybe your Power of Attorney, spouse, or designated trustee knows where this document is, in case they need to refer back to it for your health care wishes or verify documents during planning. Maybe you have a Trust. Those documents, along with any other legal documents that dictate the disposition, titling and management of your assets and healthcare should be in a logical place for your family to find, possibly a safe deposit box or a clearly marked folder in your office.

2) **Insurance Policies:** These days, due to the society we live in, we are insured up to the eyeballs, so make sure if you're paying all these premiums that you know where to find the information if and when the time comes to use it. You may have life insurance, health insurance, disability insurance, long term care, liability coverage, renter's/home-owner's insurance, car insurance, heck maybe even cell phone insurance. You may want to have the main coverage information pages clearly organized in a binder or folder for ease of reference and perhaps file them into an electronic file or email archive in case some documents go missing for when you are on the go and need to access them on the spot. Always have access to the policy number and contact phone number at a minimum, so when you call for help, they can verify you.

3) **Professionals Contact Information:** So maybe you're rolling in the big bucks and have collected an impressive array of professionals to help you with your increasingly complex life. Attorneys, accountants, CPAs, insurance agents, primary care physicians, personal bankers, and of course, financial advisors are just some to consider. This one is easier than others, as you can just add their numbers to your phone. However, make sure you have

a backup in case they have an emergency, leave the business without telling you, or for some reason are unable to be reached when you need them most. Also, make sure your next in line has their contact information or knows where to find it, and when they call on your behalf, they are authorized to speak to your advisors regarding your affairs.

4) **Title or Deed Documents:** This refers to your vehicle title, the title to your home, boat, motorcycle, and any other property where a proof of ownership applies. I've been in a situation before when I was selling a vehicle and for the life of me couldn't find the title to the car (this was in my younger, less responsible days). I turned the house upside down, and after losing the interest of that buyer for taking so long, I finally found it under the passenger seat! Don't let that happen to you. Keep all important documents in a safe place and take a picture of them in case they need to be replaced, or if that would help in conducting the business you are looking to do. I personally have a fire/waterproof safe where I store these items so if my residence burns down or floods, I don't have the additional burden of replacing vital documents via government bureaucracy.

5) **Powers of Attorney/Health Care Directive:** This expands on the first point. Yes, you want your wishes for disposition of assets and the care you will receive if incapacitated to be in writing and retrievable for your loved ones. You'll also need to have legal documents to authorize someone to act on your behalf. This especially comes into play for a Durable Power of Attorney, allowing someone to manage your financial affairs, as well as Healthcare Directive which allows someone to act on your behalf when making medical decisions for your care. For any estate planning matters and documents, you should consider working with a qualified estate planning attorney. You may want to consult with your circle of professionals. Giving them a copy of these documents may be prudent in case something happens to you.

Five Ways to Save Energy at Home

We talk a lot in this book about curbing your impulse spending and not wasting money on material things, but what about things you rarely think about but have to pay? Enter electricity bills. If you save $30 per month following these tips over the course of a year, that's a plane ticket to go somewhere you really love! Why spend more on energy when it doesn't give you direct joy? You could install solar panels, but here are some easier options.

1) **Use LED Bulbs:** Chances are, you've already updated your bulbs to CFLs, those spiral-looking bulbs. Changing lightbulbs is one of the easiest ways to save energy. LED (Light Emitting Diode) lights are very efficient. You've probably seen them on everything from Christmas lights to vehicle turn signals. Don't just look at the lights on your ceiling fans and lamps. These super bulbs can be placed in oven lights, microwave lights, refrigerators, outdoor fixtures and even nightlights. They last longer and use less energy. Some utility companies may give them to you for free, so check with yours. Yet another example of going green and saving green!

2) **Use a Power Strip:** Did you know that even if turned off, many appliances still plugged into an outlet are using energy? Why waste money on your cell phone charger or toaster if it's not being used 90% of the day? You don't have to go wild with these--just focus on the areas where you have a lot of electrical cords, such as entertainment centers (TV, DVR, stereo system) or your desk (lamp cord, cell phone charger, laptop, fan). Then, once they are all plugged in, just press the switch to turn them off when you're not using them. Power strips can also reduce the risk of damage to appliances in the event of a power surge (make sure they are identified as surge protectors) and may reduce the risk of fire, as well.

3) **Check Your Insulation:** According to the US Department of Energy, heating and cooling a home accounts for almost half the home's total energy use. *Half!* Now, if you rent your home, there is not much you can do other than ask the landlord or management company to make changes. In your own home, having proper insulation is key to maximizing the consistency of the home's temperature. Don't just think about the stuff behind your walls--there are other easy fixes, too. Look at the siding along your doors, the caulking

along windows, as well as fireplaces and exhaust fans. Some energy companies will come to your home for free or a nominal charge to perform an *Energy Audit*, informing you of all the ways you can save energy throughout your home. There are even some nonprofits that do this to help ease the strain on the grid and carbon emissions.

4) **Always Look at the EnergyStar Ratings for Appliances:** Obviously, when you're looking for new appliances, you want the sleek, top-of the line model while getting the biggest bang for your buck, right? Well, money is not just saved on the upfront price. You'll also be paying to operate that appliance. Make sure that it proudly bears the Energy Star rating, and then look at the *EnergyGuide*, a prominent yellow notice that displays what the average energy cost is for that unit as compared to the range of other models. Some new appliances also have *eco* settings or something similar designed to use less energy for less intensive tasks.

5) **Use Fans and Windows Wisely:** I know, asking you to forego air conditioning is like taking away your smartphone. You simply can't fathom how you would survive. Air conditioning certainly has its

place, such as when you have a big gathering at home and there are lots of people and tons of cooking, or on unbearably hot days. Be sure to keep your filter clean and minimize the opening of windows and doors. Other times, it may make sense to take a cold shower, change out of sweaty clothes and use good fans and the breeze Mother Nature provides to cool down your pad. This is especially true at night, when temperatures drop, and the sun goes down. The same goes for winter. Feeling cold? Bundle up! And who doesn't love an excuse to drink tea or hot chocolate?

Five Ways to Save on Utilities (Other than Energy)

These days, it seems as if our bills are higher and greater in number. Internet services, mobile phones, video streaming, subscriptions, insurance, you name it. That doesn't mean you should give other bills such as water and gas a free ride. In fact, there are a plethora of resources provided by municipalities to help you save on your bills and it also helps you go green!

1) **Install Water-Saving Fixtures:** If you live in an older home or multi-family housing (apartment/condo), chances are the water features were pre-conservation efforts and regulations. Have you ever seen those urinals in old hotels that look like bird baths? Talk about flushing money down the drain! Installing water-efficient fixtures may include an aerator for the bathroom sink, a low-flow showerhead or a water saving toilet. Turn the water off as you lather up. If you have landscaping, look into the cost-benefit of replacing your lawn for drought tolerant plants or xeriscaping. Replace an old sprinkler system with a moisture-sensing one or look into a drip system for your garden. Be sure to look into city resources

for incentives in installing water-efficient features or landscaping. Lastly, don't be that person who turns the sprinklers on in the midday heat. Early morning or evening is best to avoid wasting water. Contact your water utility to see if they provide any water saving devices, as many do. Or keep an eye out at Home and Garden shows or, one of my favorite events, Earth Day Festivals!

2) **Pit Providers against each Other:** Now, if your city provides standard services for water, gas and electricity, this may not be an option for those utilities. However, think first if you need cable, a home phone, Internet, landscaping service and pest control. Once you narrow your list down to your must-haves, shop around for the best deals. Take a screenshot or offer letter of the best price you received and send it to your current provider or others you are considering. Make sure to compare the same contract terms, duration of the price and any other benefits. This is also an opportunity to see if your local neighborhood association, alumni association, or employer discounts can give you a leg up on utility provider discounts.

3) **Hug Your Water Heater:** We all need a little love these days, right? Besides the warm and fuzzy stuff, wrapping your water heater is essential for

saving on gas costs in the winter, and in fact all year long. Do you like taking long, warm showers? Washing clothes or dishes in hot water? Mopping your tile floors with warm soapy water? All that is thanks to your water heater hard at work. Give it a break by wrapping it in an insulation blanket. According to the US Department of Energy, insulating your water heater can cut your water heating costs by up to 16% annually, paying for itself in a year or less!

4) **Give Your Clothes Dryer a Break:** Some dryers run on gas to dry your beloved clothes and depending on the size of your load and temperature, dryers can run for more than an hour to dry clothes. Want an insider tip that my grandmother taught me? Place clothes you take out of the washer on a clothesline in the backyard or balcony, harnessing the power of the sun to do the drying for you. Then, while they are still a little damp or close to dry, toss them in the dryer for 10 minutes for that soft touch and lavender scent from your eco dryer pods. Worried about the sun fading your clothes, what to do in the winter, or you live in a perpetually cloudy area? Invest in a clothes-drying rack and you can do the same thing inside. Plus, as you snuggle under the comfort of your warm home,

your clothes will also benefit from the warm air. Here is what one looks like: https://www.thespruce.com/best-clothes-drying-racks-4154471

5) **Plant some Trees:** I love trees. Just looking at them when I'm having a bad day brings me a smile. They stand tall, gently swaying in the breeze, yet are strong and protective when bad weather rolls around. They naturally filter our water, protect against floods, nurture soil, clean our air and provide habitat for many treasured species. The reasons I put trees here, though, is that they provide shade, and shade around your home means lower cooling costs! The less direct sunlight shines into your home, the more effectively you can reduce the overall temperature of your home. Trees around your house can also save water, reducing evaporation on hot days by providing shade. Some cities provide free trees for this very reason. Look into *tree distribution days* in the Spring or attend some home and garden shows or Earth Day festivals.

Five Ways to Save on Your Taxes

Fair disclosure: this is not a complete list, just a few tips I found helpful to me that I would like to share with you. I am not a tax-professional, so you should consult one to figure out which strategies are best for you and visit *irs.gov* for the most up-to-date guidelines.

1) **<u>Start a Roth IRA:</u>** The Roth is definitely one of the greatest gifts from the IRS. Yes, you don't get a deduction on your taxes for putting money in it. (I mean honestly, does the government have to dangle prizes in front of you to get you to take care of yourself?) However, the money you put in grows tax-free and you can take it out tax free after you reach 59 ½ years old. Okay, I know, you're shaking your head, thinking "Dude, that's like 30 years away. I could care less." Well, guess what? You are going to get there someday, and you'll thank me later. Especially at the beginning of your career. If you are not in a high-income tax bracket, you may not need the tax deduction for a Traditional IRA, or you can always split your contribution limit between the two. In any case, the contributions you place into your Roth are always tax and penalty free--it's the earnings that'll get ya. Plus, as long as

204 · GARY GREWAL

your account has been open for five years, you can take out $10,000 to buy a home. Other exceptions also apply, such as using earnings for a portion of unreimbursed medical expenses or medical insurance premiums while you are unemployed (subject to change).

2) **Hold Taxable Investments Long Term:** This shouldn't be an issue unless you are trying to be an active stock trader. Most of the time your investments should be held for the long term. However, some people like to play the stock market for fun or for their vacation fund, which is fine if you can handle it. If you hold investments long term, meaning one year and a day or longer, your capital gains will be taxed at the long-term rate. But if you are in a lower tax rate, it won't be higher than 15% and may even be zero percent. However, any shorter period than that and you will be taxed at the short-term rate, which is the same as your ordinary income rate. Check out this useful article on one of my recommended websites: http://www.investopedia.com/articles/personal-finance/101515/comparing-longterm-vs-shortterm-capital-gain-tax-rates.as

3) **Donate to Charity:** To me, this is one of the most humbling and exciting things I get to do. We live in a society that molds us into being consumers, buyers and customers. Well, we really don't need that much stuff, and there are a multitude of worthy causes that make our lives better. Do you love to hike? There is probably a land trust or outdoor nonprofit that helps with that. Do you love animals? Yep, there is probably a local animal rights group or shelter. I donate to multiple causes and also give a scholarship to my high school every year. Giving some money away is something that truly will make you happy, as you are enabling others to do valuable things and are making our world a better place. Plus, you may get to deduct itemized contributions off your taxes or transfer appreciated stock tax-free!

4) **Pay Qualified Expenses with Pre-Tax Dollars:** This is a big one, especially if you work for an employer who has good benefits. Do you commute to work on the light-rail? Check out your HR benefits for the ability to contribute pre-tax dollars from your payroll into a commuter benefits account. Your employer may also offer the ability to make pre-tax contributions for childcare, parking, wellness programs and retirement health care savings

plans (RHSPs). If you also have a high-deductible retirement plan, you can also contribute to an HSA, or *Health Savings Account*. Most employers will put money into an HSA if you have the high-deductible plan, and that money should be excluded from your gross income. Your contributions into your HSA are pre-tax, they grow tax-free, and if used for eligible medical expenses, there are no taxes for distributions!

5) **Move:** If you're mobile, looking for a change of scenery, or just want to get a geographically specific job, you might consider moving to a state that is more tax-friendly than where you currently are. Currently, states such as Florida and Tennessee have no state income tax. Obviously, they have to make that up somewhere, whether it is in sales tax or property tax, so choose wisely. As you begin searching for a job, keep those receipts. Many job-search expenses may be deductible, such as travel expenses related to a job out of state or staffing agency expenses. Once you've chosen your location and found a job, it's time to move. Again, keep those receipts, as hiring movers and paying for gas and lodging when travelling to your new home may be eligible expenses.

Five Ways to Save on Attending a Tradeshow/Conference

I attended my first big kid, real-world conference when I was 22, six months into my first job out of college--and boy was it eye opening. Conferences and tradeshows are full of energy, and everyone is usually happy because they are away from their desk in a new city for a few days and get to enjoy good food, a change in pace and they have a chance to bond with their colleagues. Whatever career you are in, look for conferences in your line of work. You'll meet remarkable people, learn what's around the corner in your industry, and expand your understanding of career options you may never have known existed.

1) <u>**Check out the Website for Scholarship/Volunteer Opportunities**</u>: Not only is this going to get you a big discount (or even a free entry!) into the event, but you get a much more interactive, behind-the-scenes experience. At one conference for which I volunteered, I got to be the announcer for the bingo that was drawn every hour during the expo sessions. Apparently, I did a good enough job that I was approached by another event organizer who asked if I could do the same at their conference and apply for the scholarship. Some conferences

request you work a certain number of hours for whatever discount or complimentary pass you receive. It's a small price to pay for the ability to attend.

2) **Email the Conference Organizers to See if You can Work the Event:** If there are no scholarship options or volunteer positions listed, try emailing the event organizers to see if they could use some extra hands to help out during the event. This works even better if you know someone on the committee or can be referred to them. (Hello, LinkedIn!) While your chances are modest with this approach, since most large conferences hire event teams to help out, sometimes just the initiative you express can impress the event organizers. You can do coat check, expo set up, badge collection, program distribution or set up sponsor tables at dinner. This also is a great way to put yourself in a position of forced conversation with several attendees. It's a better way to introduce yourself and network than trying to sheepishly elbow your way to that person you've been meaning to talk to all day only to have them be pulled away by someone else.

3) **Check if Your Affiliation to any Groups can Score You a Free Pass or Discount:** There are a multitude of professional and social organizations that may provide you with some kind of discount for attending an event they put on themselves or are associated with. For example, if you're into architecture or commercial real estate, there is the U.S. Green Building Council. Or maybe you are a member of the American Psychological Association. Whichever industry you are in, being a member of these groups can often afford you a discount to a conference or even access to exclusive sessions, welcome receptions and perks such as free continuing education for your credentials.

4) **Contact the Exhibitors:** So, none of the above options have worked. What are you going to do now? Try contacting some of the companies that are sponsoring the conference. Most conference websites have a list of sponsors and exhibitors on their website, so see if they need assistance. You never know--someone may cancel last minute, and they need extra help to man the booth during the tradeshow, distribute programs during their sponsored dinner or enthusiastically gather email addresses of attendees for follow-up after the conference.

5) **Book Early and See if Your Company will Help:** Most conferences offer an early bird rate if you book early. I have seen them as high as 25%. That's $250 off a $1000 conference pass! You can also score deals by booking through their hotel partners, as they often book blocks or whole floors for the conference. Also, check out the benefits at your company. Many have professional development reimbursement policies, so you might be able to make a case to your boss. If he/she has authority over the department/company budget, you can also make the case of promising new clients, media exposure, industry insights you can share with colleagues, etc. If you are convincing enough, he/she may not only help you pay the conference fee, but hotel, travel and daily expenses, as well. Better yet, you may even be on the clock while you attend, saving your vacation days!

Five Ways to Save on Festivals and Events

Our culture is increasingly supporting spending money on experiences rather than material possessions. This is also mentioned in one of my favorite books, *Happy Money*, which I mentioned in the *Five Best Books* section. While some festivals are free and enjoyable, such as community parades, concerts in the park or movie night under the sky, the more exuberant ones featuring celebrities or desirable perks will cost you.

1) **Volunteer:** Many events, especially if they are put on by nonprofit groups, will seek volunteers to reduce the ever-increasing costs of event staff. You might be selling tickets, checking IDs, setting up/manning booths, being a vendor liaison, helping out with hospitality, or my favorite, helping out with greening/recycling efforts. Even if the event website does not explicitly state they are looking for volunteers, it pays to email the event organizers directly and show your passion for helping out. I can speak from experience that this worked out a few times, and I didn't just get into the event for free. I ate free, made friends, got a ton of swag and useful giveaways, and best of all, got access to

areas of the festival few ever get to see. Persistence pays off!

2) **Eat Beforehand or bring Your Own Food:** I would always suggest eating something before the event if you can. Festival food is usually not the healthiest, nor is it fun to pay $14 for a chicken sandwich that tastes like rubber between two cotton balls. Now, if you want to splurge and try some of the festival food, make sure you bring cash. Sometimes the vendors will charge extra or have a minimum order amount in order for them to cover the cost of credit card processing fees. If the festival allows, try to bring your own food, as well. These should be items that are nutrient dense, don't require preparation, and are small in size so you can stuff them in your purse or cinch bag. Examples include protein bars, an apple/banana, nut butter packets, trail mix, peanuts, etc. Oh, and most importantly, don't forget your reusable water bottle! *I just love paying $5 for a bottle of lukewarm water*, said no one ever.

3) **Go on the Last Day:** Sometimes the tickets are less expensive, especially if you go straight to the box office or entrance. The real savings though, happen when you are inside. Vendors typically budget

a certain amount of supplies. Depending on how busy it was over the weekend, they may have over-stocked. This can mean free or discounted food, T-shirts, gifts, swag, entrance to separately ticketed events, less waiting in line, etc. This has been my experience, so if you can pull it off, go for it!

4) **Go toward the End of the Day:** I mean, if you can go on the last day at the end of the day, it's a double win! Now why would you want to go at the end of the day? Won't I be rushed at spending time at the event, you ask? I'm not saying go 20 minutes before the event is over, but maybe two hours. You can also find a list of vendors and a map of the festival or stages/areas that are of interest to you beforehand, so you can make a beeline for the places that are important to you. The best part about going at the end of the day is the gatekeepers and security typically cut off ticketing towards the end of the day, as they don't anticipate anyone else coming, and this has enabled me to be ushered into events without even taking out my wallet.

5) **Keep an Eye on the Event Social Media Pages:** This is where you will find announcements of volunteers needed, news, updates, cancellations, etc.

What you will also find is coupon codes, contests and giveaways for doing things such as liking the page, sharing it, posting a picture, and more. You can score some free tickets and other bonuses simply for keeping track. What else will you find? Let's say that someone bought tickets a while ago and can no longer go. They will likely post that they have X number of tickets available, plus VIP access, plus food/drink tickets, etc. If you see this and contact them in a timely manner, you can save a decent amount of dough. Another reason to keep an eye on the social media page? Let's say you go and lose something. Most worthy people will post what they found on the event page, and if you find it "such as an umbrella, sunglasses, or worse, your wallet) you just saved yourself some money!

Five Relationships
to have to Save Money

Now let's get this straight. I'm not saying go hang out at the ticket counter at the airport and ask for the gate agent's number to get lunch sometime just for the sole intention of using them for their connections. What I am saying is if you already have a connection in some of these fields (this list, like others, is non-inclusive), then it might pay to be extra nice to them or offer them your own perk, so it feels more like a two-way street.

1) **A Friend Who Works for an Airline:** We all know those friends who brag about travelling so much for work that they rack up enough points for free flights to Hawaii every year. Well, the next best thing is knowing someone who can maybe give you some free buddy passes like they do on Southwest, or maybe if you're best friends/dating someone, you can fly free with them all year. Even if they can't give you free flights, they can probably give you tips on when to buy your tickets, when to volunteer your seat for delay perks or even change your flight or throw your bags on for free. If you become friends with someone like this or they do you a favor, it pays dividends to thank

them appropriately and reciprocate, such as giving them a gift card to their favorite restaurant when they throw you a freebie.

2) **A Friend Who Works for a Hotel Company:** Depending on where you are staying, any seasoned traveler knows hotels can be the second, if not the most, expensive part of any vacation. A hotel in Downtown Denver can easily cost you $300, versus a motel in Canton, Ohio which costs you less than a tank of gas. As you travel, be on the friendly side of the people who check you in, carry your bags or help you with any part of your stay. If your cousin Mike's girlfriend works for some trendy hotel chain, maybe she can add some extra points to your loyalty program to a free stay, upgrade you to the best room, throw in free breakfast or a courtesy car voucher, you name it. Luckily, I have some friends in this business and have been able to obtain all of the previously mentioned perks at various times, and they keep coming because I reciprocate, such as letting them crash at my place for free.

3) **Someone in a Job/Company where You want to Work One Day:** This may not save you money per se (but maybe a raise!). However, if you have your

eye on some new startup or the most coveted architecture firm in town, you want to get on the
inside. Go to conferences or networking events
they attend. Find out where they volunteer. Find
out where they go for happy hour or team events.
Heck--hang out in their lobby pretending to read
this book, so that the next time some workers
come down for a break, you can introduce yourself. From there, you can ask how they got the job,
what their interview advice is, what their managers look for, etc. If you do your homework, not
only can you snag the job, you can negotiate the
salary as you have inside information from a current employee.

4) **A Friend Who Works for a Promotion/Events
Company:** You'll really come to like this one if
you're the YOLO type, or just love concerts and VIP
events. One of my friends in college worked for a
promotion company, and we always got on the
guest list for the cool parties that other students
had to pay for AND wait forever in line to get into.
Maybe they can score you free (comp) tickets, get
you into the best seats or give you a wristband for
all you can eat catering in the VIP area. They can
get you in and get you the perks. But don't be a
mooch. As with anything, friendships like these

are cultivated over time, and gratitude is key. There is nothing worse than having to deal with nagging friends about getting free stuff from you, like it's a mouth you can't feed fast enough. Next time you get perks from your friends, invite them out for drinks and dinner. Show them love and you'll be good.

5) **Someone Who is Good with Cars/Home Repairs:** Don't you just jump for joy when your dishwasher stops working? Home and car repairs are on the top of the list for the most annoying inconveniences. They disrupt your schedule/comfort and may cost thousands of dollars that you do not have. (Keep working on that six-month emergency fund!) If you are handy with fixing things at home, then by all means do it yourself. Or have a barbeque and treat your contractor friend Tony like royalty. Then, as you are cleaning up in the kitchen, you can moan about your inoperable dishwasher, to which Tony will (hopefully!) say, "Oh, let me have a look." Ta-da! He feels like a hero, and you don't have to spend all night doing the dishes. Send him home with leftovers and offer him something in return, like offering to help clean out his garage.

Five Things to Look for when Considering a New City

Americans these days are more mobile than ever. Whether you are a new college grad who accepted a job offer in New York City, trying to get away from increasing congestion or just want a fresh start, there are a number of factors to consider when thinking about where to pitch your flag. Don't make the decision based on emotionally compelling Instagram pictures. Look at these tips instead!

1) **Cost of Living:** Obvious as it is, this is what you must look for, as it directly impacts your bottom line. What's included in cost of living? Think of rent/home prices, the cost of gas, groceries, taxes, beer, dentist visits--you name it. Are wages decent and do they afford you a good lifestyle? One of the largest expenses you will incur is probably housing. However, you also have to consider what you will be earning at a high-cost city versus a low-cost small town and whether you'll be employed or be a business owner. Sure, the weather in Knoxville TN is not the same as Laguna Beach CA, but maybe you'll be able to live peacefully and afford a comfortable lifestyle instead of sweating over debt and expenses.

2) **Major Industries:** There are a few reasons this is important. First, major industries or companies in the city you are looking into provide jobs--hopefully good paying ones. This means you or your family have good employment prospects, the workers will earn a living and have money to spend doing business with you, tax revenue is steady, and it provides swift demand for housing and keeping values up. Typically, you'll want to look for companies that have set down roots, not those that will jump at the next state who offers them tax breaks and move all 10,000 employees. Universities, hospitals and state and local government typically provide for steady employment and are dedicated to their location versus some corporations, manufacturing and natural resources employers who may be more sensitive to cyclical conditions in the economy.

3) **Infrastructure Investments:** Does the city you're considering have strong leadership guiding its path? Are the citizen's concerns aligned with that of local government? Look for cities that are investing money towards sustaining growth. This means efficient roadways, commuter rail systems, bike lanes and bikeways, trails, parks, libraries,

schools, community gathering spots, etc. If well planned and executed, infrastructure investments can be a boon to cities in terms of business investment and real estate values. People want to live in communities with good schools, safe places for recreation, dependable options for transit and in essence seeing their tax dollars in ways that improve their lives. If you look at cities that have experienced substantial growth these last several years, they all have some type of infrastructure overhaul plans.

4) **Migration Patterns:** Have people been moving out of the city or into it? While this facet is not the most important, migration patterns tell a story. If the population has been decreasing over the last five years, is crime getting worse? Is the local government turning a blind eye to deteriorating schools or fleeing businesses? At the same time, when a city has been experiencing large inflows, is it due to infrastructure investment? Good weather or quality of life? Studying migration patterns can help you understand if the cities are going to be successful in the long term or if they are on road to desolation. For example, if you buy a home, what will happen to your home value when you

decide to move again to be closer to family or a new opportunity? Speaking of which...

5) **Real Estate Values:** This is kind of included in cost of living, but what we're talking about here is the trends of real estate values, not what they are at the point of time in which you are moving. Does real estate hold its value? If you look over the last 10 or 20 years, what's been the movement of real estate prices? If you look back at the housing crash of the late 2000's, homes in desirable communities with good schools, enviable locations and low crime tended to hold their values through the tumultuous crash better than those in new suburbs on the outskirts of town or those in neighborhoods where it never really turned around. If real estate fluctuates too much, this should factor into your decision on how long you plan on staying there and if you can stomach the loss in equity which may occur. Even if you plan on holding your property through tough times, will you be able to retain a renter to cover your costs?

Five Questions to Ask Your Realtor when Shopping for a Home

No newsflash here. Buying a home is probably the largest purchase you will make in your life. Thus, you'll want to be represented by the best. Look for a real estate agent with integrity, thirst for negotiation, and someone who will go to bat for you when things go awry, as they often do in these kinds of transactions. Don't just go off sales and referrals. Hire a real estate agent like you would a real job candidate.

1) **If I Called Your Last Client Right Now, how would They Describe Their Experience?** You want a candid account from their perspective, but also to see if they gloat about their success while stating everything went according to plan. You want someone whom you feel is honest and can own up to making mistakes. Also, they should tell you something they are going to do better next time. A driven real estate agent should always strive to improve.

2) **What other Properties/Clients will You also be Pursuing while Working with Me?** If the real estate agent is trying to take on as many clients as

224 · GARY GREWAL

possible, this should be a red flag, especially if your price range is at the lower end of what they usually work with. Think about it--if the agent has 20 clients and they are mostly in the $500K+ range while you are looking at $300K, who do you think they are going to spend more time with or do research for? If they are new and still building their client base, chances are they are going to work hard for you, so you'll give them a good testimonial or referrals, and they need to get some closings under their belt.

3) **How would you Handle a Situation where You Represent Me as well as the Seller?** This is another key point, because if they are representing the seller, won't they want to get the very best price possible for them, for a higher commission and happy client? That won't fare as well for you. Typically, there is a clause in the contract when this situation happens, such as reducing commission or bringing in a third party. Make sure you understand it thoroughly and are comfortable with having your real estate agent represent both sides, if that situation happens.

4) <u>**What Warning Signs Do You Look for when doing a Walkthrough of the Home/Showing?**</u> You want someone who has a decent knowledge of a quality home and can easily identify problem spots. They don't need to be an architect in their sleep; however, they should have a keen eye for things such as water damage, faulty electrical systems, rust and corrosion, cheap cosmetic "renovations," etc. Not only can this save you money in case things have been covered up, but you can also have more leverage when negotiating the price. If the real estate agent is clueless on these things and is only focused on submitting an offer, find someone else who has your best interests in mind and will point out potential issues with the property than you can use to lower the price or have the seller fix beforehand.

5) <u>**What Fees/Closing Costs can You Help Me Negotiate into the Contract?**</u> As you may know, along with the down payment, there are several closing costs. *Save BIG* by Elizabeth Leamy, part of the *Five Books to Read* chapter, outlines some of the closing costs that are easier to negotiate than others. While you may not be able to negotiate the appraisal fee since it is typically required by the lender, other fees, such as the HOA document

preparation fee, can be negotiated, waived or paid by the seller. The negotiable fees can also depend heavily on if it is a seller's market versus buyer's market. If it is a seller's market, as it is now as I write this in Denver, some buyers are even allowing the sellers to stay in their home rent free for a few months on top of paying above asking price and all closing costs! With the prevalence of people posting about their home buying experiences online, you should be able to get a decent idea of what you can negotiate depending on what market you are in.

Five Ways to Save Money when Buying a Home

While some of this information is my own knowledge and research from sites such as *Bankrate.com*, *Investopedia.com* and *Zillow.com*, many of these key tips came from one of my favorite books (#5 on the *Five Books to Read* chapter), which is *Save BIG* by Elizabeth Leamy. I highly recommend reading it if you plan to shop for home soon.

1) **Put Down a 20% Down Payment:** Look. Buying a house is probably the biggest purchase you are ever going to make. Unless you are going to try your hand at flipping and buying up houses with nothing down in an attempt to sell and make more, it makes sense to put 20% down. You'll save hundreds per month by not paying private mortgage insurance and perhaps qualifying for a better rate or less fees. Now, if you are funneling all your savings into your house fund, you're going to want to beef it up to more than 20% to include closing costs, home repairs, liens and the list goes on. Plus, don't forget you always need an emergency fund.

2) **Negotiate Closing Costs:** Just because there are a bunch of confusing and official-sounding fees on a lender's formal documents does not mean they are all valid. The application fee, administration fees and the appraisal review fee are just some of the ones about which you can question your lender. You need to understand each fee and its reason. Shop around for title insurance and see which ones have the most reasonable fees. Ask your friends who have recently bought homes how their experience was with their loan officer and what fees they were able to wiggle out of. While negotiating closing costs is typically easier in a buyer's market, some sellers who have multiple offers may be willing to throw in some cash toward your closing costs to seal the deal sooner than later.

3) **Buy a Home in the Winter:** Think about all the people with children and how they don't want to switch them out during the school year, as well as all the people who want to shop when the weather is nice so they can envision their pool parties and what color to paint the bathrooms with the light shining in. According to *Save BIG*, November to February is ideal. There may be less homes on the market and so you will have less choices.

However, finding the house you want during these months can save you a great deal on the house if the sellers have less interest in the colder months and are more willing to negotiate on price, contingencies or closing costs.

4) **Get Three Good Faith Estimates (GFE):** This is vital. After October 2015, the GFE was replaced by the *Loan Estimate* and *Closing Disclosure Form*. The Loan Estimate must be provided to you within three days of applying for a loan. It provides a breakdown of fees, rates, terms, and other information regarding the loan for your home. (Remember those fees I suggested you negotiate?) Then, at least three days before closing, the lender needs to provide you with a Closing Disclosure Form, which is basically the same as a Loan Estimate, except it lists who is paying for what (buyer, lender, seller, etc.). Is there a prepayment penalty? If you can, get these from your banker, one from a broker, and one from a mortgage lender. Compare them side by side to be sure which fees are standard and which may be flexible. For more on this, see: https://www.zillow.com/mortgage-learning/tila-respa-disclosures-trid/

5) **<u>Don't Skip the Home Inspection:</u>** While you may want to say *no thanks* to the warranties offered to you, except the all-important *First Year Warranty*, the home inspection is crucial--especially if buying an older home. Is there mold where you can't see it? Are the baseboards under the sink in the laundry room rotting? Is there a leak in the roof that you can't see if you are touring the home in summer? (Another reason to shop in winter!) It is well worth your investment to know what you are getting into. If there are issues, you can stick it to the seller to pay for the repairs or ask for a credit for underlying issues that may be a problem. By the way, you can also negotiate among different home inspectors!

Five Mistakes to Avoid
as a First-Time Homebuyer

I said it once and I'll say it again--your home is probably the biggest purchase you will make, so prepare yourself as best you can! Get multiple opinions from industry leaders, talk to friends and family who have bought houses for advice and use Mother Google. It's exciting to buy a home, and you might be itching to post a picture of you jumping in front of your new crib like the rest of your friends, but do it in a manner where you'll be able to sleep at night knowing you prepared as best as you could.

1) **Comparing Your Rent to just the Mortgage Payment:** The first thing to note, if you don't already, is that principle plus interest is not the only costs when owning a home and you cannot compare that to your rent. There are also property taxes, homeowners insurance and if applicable, HOA fees and mortgage insurance. This is especially important in states that have high property taxes, or in condo buildings where the monthly HOA is around $500 per month to cover the pool, fitness center, trash removal, etc. Get an accurate compilation of the monthly charges you will face and

then compare that to the rent and see if it is feasible with your cash flow situation.

2) **Not being Preapproved:** This is almost like walking into a job interview without a resume or cover letter. You've got to show the real estate agents, sellers and other involved parties that you are the real deal, not some tire kicker who likes to tour homes as a way to pass time on a Sunday afternoon. In order to be preapproved, you generally need to be prequalified first. If you have a letter stating the banks believe you are able to afford a $350,000 home and would be willing to extend a loan to you, this makes you more agile to make a serious offer on a home when you find the right one. Plus, it'll prevent you from scrambling to gather tax statements and other documents when you find the house you want, as by the time all that is done, the house may already be under contract.

3) **Not Talking to the Neighbors:** This is important, as the websites only show you the factual aspects of the home such as construction material, square footage and type of flooring. If you are going to be living there, though, don't you want to know about neighborhood dynamics? Is speeding a problem? Are most homes owner-occupied?

Talking to the neighbors, especially those with a track record, can help you understand trends in the neighborhood and troubles which may fly under the radar or the real estate agent. While it's doubtful a fraternity will move right next door to you, there are plenty of nightmares that ring true for some people who are their actual neighbors.

4) **Skipping the Home Warranty:** Even if your place is relatively new, you want to keep in mind that anything can go wrong given the circumstances. Whether your garage door opener fries out, your sprinkler system breaks, or the upstairs shower basin springs a plumbing leak, you'll want to have yourself covered. A home warranty may seem like an easy way to knock off a few hundred dollars off your closing costs. However, it can pay for itself many times over by fixing just a few things. Make sure you know what exactly your policy covers and any contingencies or clauses it has.

5) **Overestimating Your Commitment to the Home/Area:** Many people become emotionally attached to a home, sometimes going as far to say, "It was love at first sight." Sure, you can imagine drinking wine on the balcony with your future spouse, or how your future kids will love playing in

the big, open backyard. Sometimes our vision into the future with a home can cause us to justify over-paying for a property, since we claim we'll be there for a while. The next thing you know, a layoff, di-vorce, a family health issue or some other issue will cause you to uproot and sell. Housing prices don't always go up, so you may end up selling at a loss after considering all the closing/moving costs. Or, if you can't afford to sell, you may end up being an inadvertent landlord, which is also something for which to prepare.

Five Ways to Save
on Moving Expenses

Buying a home and moving go hand in hand, and it's easy to shove your budget aside when you're stressed about moving, escrow, closing costs, packing, etc. The best way is to prepare as much in advance as possible. If you know you are going to move, pare down your belongings, plan some time off and allow wiggle room in your schedule to move. Moving can either be stressful or adventurous. It's all in how you approach it!

1) **<u>Check with Local Retailers for Boxes:</u>** While going to big box stores increasingly seems to be an activity of the past, they can still be gold mines for finding new, clean and sturdy boxes. Most of the inventory you see on the shelves at Target or Safeway comes in larger boxes for ease of transport. If you need larger boxes, consider a home furnishings store such as Bed Bath and Beyond or an electronics store. Try to go in the morning just after they would have received the load, so the boxes have not been broken down or taken away by the recycling hauler already. Some stores do their inventory and stocking overnight, so call and ask when the best chance is to score some free

boxes and packaging, too. This one step can easily save you over $100, depending on the number of boxes you need.

2) **Move on Your Own:** Hiring movers isn't cheap, that's for sure. The average price of hiring a mover is $25-$50 per hour, according to *HomeAdvisor*. To top that off, some customers even hire a company to pack their belongings for them! Understandably, if you have a large family or young children and not a lot of time, you may need to hire help. However, if your family is able to help move, it can save substantial cash. When my family moved to a new home in 2010, I packed up everything over the course of six weeks and it wasn't too bad. Luckily, we had my uncle and several other family members who came to help load things into the truck and take smaller boxes in their cars. Treat those who help to dinner and they are happy, as true family and friends will jump at the chance to show you their loyalty.

3) **Clean Out, Organize, Dispose:** There are a few benefits to this concept. Getting rid of items you no longer need, use or want can generate some cash by selling them on Craigslist, in a garage sale or on one of several apps. Also, the less stuff you

move means less boxes needed, less time spent on packing and less items to move when the time comes. Decluttering in general is healthy for you, as moving is one of the only times you are forced to go through all of your belongings, move all of your furniture and actually recognize the contents of your drawers and cabinets. You're starting a new chapter when you move, so do away with things that no longer have much value or utility in your life. In fact, moving is also a great time to gather old clothes, books, and dishes for donation purposes. Perhaps someone else can benefit from what you no longer need, and once you settle into your new digs, you'll feel a sense of relief.

4) **Optimize Your Move-In/Move-Out Dates:** Let's be real. If you are taking possession of two places at once, even for a few nights, you are wasting money. If your lease ends on the 12th, make sure you are in your new place and out of the old one by the 12th. It helps to have your move in/out day on a weekend or a day off, so you can get it all done at once. In my experience, the place you are moving out of will give you some leniency, such as a 48-hour grace period from when your lease ends to when the final walkthrough and inspection occur. If you are selling or buying a home, these

timelines can get a little messier, as you are depending on the closing date, which is affected by mortgage funding, inspection, appraisal, counter offers, etc. Try your best to build in a grace period such as a 30-day lease back, so you can have a month to find a new place to live if your home actually sells.

5) **If You must Hire, Shop Around:** Okay, so you're going to splurge and hire movers to do the heavy lifting for you (no pun intended). At least do yourself a favor and shop around, as you would any other service. Beware, though, not to look only for price, such as cost per hour. Look for reviews on *Yelp, Google, HomeAdvisor,* or *Houzz.* Ask around. Ask them for references which you can validate. Know their insurance policies for damaged belongings. Sure, you may not pay the absolute lowest for movers. However, keep in mind they are pretty much moving everything you own, including Grandma's Victorian lamp set and your brand-new flat screen. So, choose wisely. If you want to save money, you can move the little things yourself in your own car and hire movers to move the larger items.

Five Ways to Save on Your Home Renovation

Have you seen those memes online that show a picture of weekends in your 20's of partying on a boat with a bunch of friends and then below it shows weekends in your 30's with a picture of a guy sadly walking into Home Depot? Ah, the joys of getting older, adulting and buying your own place. Eventually, you'll want to make some changes to make it your own or just more comfortable to live in, and home renovations are not cheap. Read on to save!

1) **Buy Materials Yourself:** Costco is a great resource for this, no joke. I've seen bulk cabinets, backsplashes, wall tiles and even flooring. Best of all, they sometimes have member pricing and discounts with garage cabinet companies, whole kitchen remodels and other projects via their services or roadshows that they have in the store. Another idea is simply to search online for what you need, such as *quartz countertops wholesale* and you can find some outlets in your area that are open to the public. Maybe they are trying to get rid of some inventory to make room for the new trendy stuff and will give you a discount to haul it away. Not only can you save costs by buying the

materials yourself, if your contractor doesn't have to spend time hauling it, you may save on the labor costs, as well. Lastly, keep an eye out for Home and Garden shows in your area. Many times, contractors and vendors have *Show-Only Specials* from built-in barbecues to stone pavers. You may be able to get good deals on entire renovation projects, as well!

2) **Volunteer for the Demolition/Hauling:** This hits at the idea of reducing labor costs. If you are redoing a bathroom, for example, ask your prospective contractors how much they would reduce the cost of the project if you tore out all of the old tile and hauled it out on your own. This is a case where having a pickup, or knowing someone who does, pays off. You can haul the debris to a local construction waste/recycling facility or Materials Recovery Facility (MRF). If you don't, you can still let off some steam and save money by swinging at that old tile, ripping up some flooring or tearing out old drywall--as long as you know what you are doing and don't end up busting a plumbing line!

3) **Search for Excess Materials at other Construction Sites:** This might be easier if you live in a developing area with commercial and residential

construction nearby, but also simply keep an eye out for construction trucks, roadside dumpsters and other signs that construction is going on. You may even check on new home developments across town, as they buy their building material in bulk, and after cutting a block of quartz, leave it for disposal. You can also try calling construction company offices and building construction supply companies to see if they know where that kind of material ends up going.

4) **Invest in Focal Points:** There is a reason some home renovations genuinely add resale value to your home and others don't. Think about what you notice when you tour a home. Fresh paint, eye-catching landscaping, new door and garage door, shiny hardwood floors and countertops. Then there are things that you didn't really pay attention to in the 20 minutes you spent at the open house. Things like the towel racks in the bathroom from Restoration Hardware or the crown molding in the closet. New windows and a water heater are nice and add to efficiency, but most experts will tell you they don't carry their weight in adding to a home's value. Consult with those in your circle who work in contracting, real estate or interior design. Search online for articles and forums and

look up pictures of homes that met or exceeded their asking price in your range. What did they add that you can replicate in an economical manner? Little things can go a long way in adding to the *wow factor* of your home.

5) **Consider Refinishing before Replacing:** Of course, this isn't the most attractive option (unless you thrive on saving cash like I do) but try to see your home in a new light. Are your cabinets truly falling apart or do they just look dull? Is your carpet putrid and torn or just needing some good old shampooing? From bathroom fixtures to lighting and more, you may just need to look into polishing the brass sconces, sanding your cabinets or cleaning the grout and polishing the floor tiles. You'll find this is not only less expensive than full-on replacement, but also less burdensome, and you're not tearing apart your home and disrupting your life. Try just a few things and see how you feel, and you'll start to love your new digs. YouTube and HGTV shows are very resourceful for finding some refinishing ideas!

Five Ways to Save
on the Dating Scene

Ah, the courtship dance known as dating. From middle school dances to swiping on our phones while we ride the subway, dating has evolved. Some might argue it's gotten more complicated than crushing on the boy/girl down the street. Others say with the advent of social media, people have to compete with their amazing date nights and exotic restaurant experiences. Here are some ways to find true love, save money and maybe reveal the gold digger in the person you're exploring.

1) **Go on an Art Walk/Museum Free Day:** Not only can this be free/pretty cheap, but you can also determine the cultural intellect of your date. Many museums have free days for the community to check them out, usually provided by a sponsoring company or your library. Being free probably means more people will be there, but that can soften the awkwardness when you ask your date what they think about abstract expressionism and they say something completely off-topic. Check out the visitor's bureau website for art walks and different museums near you.

2) **Go Hiking:** Get in a workout, immerse yourself in nature AND pay nothing for a date? What could be better? You may be thinking this is overkill, and it probably is, for a first date, anyway. However, once you've moved past the obligatory dinner/drinks date, hiking is a great option. You may find out your date hates exercise/the outdoors and thus you'll save yourself the duty of breaking it off with them. You can choose strenuous hikes or easy ones. Hikes provide the chance for you to chat while being periodically interrupted by beautiful vistas and friendly hikers. Plus, when you get to the turnaround/peak, it's a great time to impress him/her with your homemade snacks and have a heartfelt conversation while overlooking a sea of pine trees and granite peaks (or landfills and trailer parks, whatever you have in your backyard).

3) **Happy Hour is Your Friend:** So maybe this is the first date, or you don't want your date to be weirded out by these other options, so you go the typical dinner/drinks route. Rule #1: Don't go on the weekend. Rule #2: Go during happy hour. Some places have unflattering discounts, but do your research and you can find deals such as half off drinks, $5 tacos, flatbreads, etc. That's where you'll save money and have your pick of where you

want to sit. Also, it may provide an easy escape in case the date goes south fast. "Oh, I forgot. I have to go buy a cake for my coworker's birthday before that one bakery closes!"

4) **Go to a Free Festival:** Festivals aren't just for summer. Think about Pumpkin Harvest Festivals, Halloween Parades, Christmas marketplaces, Winter Wonderland, Blood Orange Festivals--you get the idea. An easy Google search will show you any number of events going on in your area. In addition to providing a calm atmosphere to generate conversation without uncomfortably staring at each other at a dinner, festivals also provide intermittent focus points for stimulating further conversation. "Oh, look at that life-sized ice sculpture of Martha Stewart!" Festivals are a nice way to enjoy the environment around you without having to do much planning to make sure the date isn't utterly boring.

5) **Try an Outdoor Music Festival/Movie Night:** So, I'm separating free festivals from music festivals as they probably cost money, and also may not provide the most opportunity for a quiet conversation. That being said, if during conversation with your date you uncover their taste in music, art, or

cinema, you can suggest an outdoor movie or music festival. I'm not saying blow $5,000 taking them to Ultra and rage for three days straight, but maybe there is a music showcase for local artists you can support or a music festival that's fundraising for some cause in your city. It'll definitely show your noble side, bonus points for you! Movie nights are great too, as it provides for side-by-side conversation along with a family-friendly movie going on for distraction. Many cities put on free movie nights at parks and art venues. Who knows, maybe it'll bring you both together through feelings of nostalgia. Either way, it's free, so no loss if it doesn't work out.

Five Tips to Help
You Manage Your Debt

Debt is the anchor that can hold you back in your finances. If you don't use it carefully, it can sink your ship. Other than mortgage debt, you should avoid going into any kind of debt. If you are in that debt, it should be your priority to pay it off. This includes auto loans, credit cards and even student loans. I'm not a big fan of large student loans, especially with the recent explosion of student debts and how certain degrees are not truly coming to the rescue with high income. If you must use debt to attain your goals, please be strategic and consider the options below.

1) **Consolidate to a Lower Interest Rate:** This isn't always an option, but let's say you have a student loan or medical loan from related subsidiaries or owned by the same financial institution. You may be able to move balances from a higher interest rate to that with a lower one. Not only can this reduce excessive interest rate payments that do little to lower your overall debt balance, it can also make it easier to manage and track so you're less likely to

miss a payment or become overwhelmed by how many loans to track.

2) **Pay Off the Highest Interest Rate/Smallest Balance First:** When you look at your debts, think about what you feel is more meaningful for you. If you pay off the highest interest rate loan first, you'll reduce the amount of money being thrown away to the debtor. Then, as your remaining loan payments are reduced, it might help you frame a mindset of how the debt is manageable, and you are making solid progress. On the other hand, let's say you have a loan of $1200, $8,000 and $15,000. Try to kill off that small loan first so you can say to yourself, you've paid off one of three loans. This will help motivate you beyond just making minimum payments and the mindset of defeat, to that of knocking them out one at a time. Baby steps will help you conquer the overall goal!

3) **Set Up Recurring Monthly Payments:** Similar to how I recommend automating regular savings and retirement contributions, you should also set up recurring payments to your debt so that the balance and interest don't creep up on you. Once you have a three-month cash cushion for monthly expenses, focus on paying down debt before you sock other savings away. Typically, this is a

guaranteed rate of return of 3-20% of whatever your loan interest rates are. Don't fall into the trap of how next month you won't eat out as much, so you'll save more. As you know, this leads to nothing or very little servicing on loan payments. Figure out your fixed expenses, leave a buffer of $100-$200 dollars for the occasional night out or birthday gift, and whatever is left over should be designated to recurring payments for debt and savings.

4) **Negotiate Lower Rate/Balance Forgiveness:** Negotiating is an excellent tool, because it can make principal loan amounts completely disappear without taking anything out of your pocket. I haven't seen this done yet for student loans, but anything is possible these days. With medical payments, auto loans, personal loans and others, it may be possible to have them reduced or forgiven. Many lenders would rather get something back from you rather than take on the administrative burden of hiring a collections agency to hunt you down. As far as the rate, you can make the case to the lender of how you have been improving your credit, haven't missed a payment and can even make larger payments if they reduce your interest rate. It never hurts to ask, and as much as it seems every

bank is out there to ruin you, some are under-standing, especially if you are a loyal customer and they want to build that good customer experience for you.

5) **<u>Check into Loan Forgiveness Programs:</u>** I have seen these programs mainly for student loans, though others may exist, as well. I had a friend who joined the Peace Corps, and one of my old roommates joined an underserved community clinic to get his dental school loans forgiven. Whether it is military service, starting a nonprofit, or joining Teach for America, there are ways to get some or even all of your loans forgiven. *NerdWallet* provides a decent breakdown of the options, as does the Department of Education: https://studentaid.ed.gov/sa/repay-loans/forgiveness-cancellation/public-service

Five Ways to Earn Extra Cash

Okay, so you're tired of reading of all the ways you have to cut costs or budget. "What else do you want me to do, stop buying toilet paper!?" Well, no, that's just not hygienic. With the explosion of social media, the sharing economy, freelancing and more, there are countless ways to earn extra dollars and maybe even blossom into a full-time career. Here are some ways to earn extra cash so you can spend on things you care about or save more toward a vacation.

1) **Rent Out Vacant Space:** Airbnb, anyone? Today there are so many ways to get extra cash by simply putting what you are not using on the marketplace. If you live by yourself, can you live with a roommate? Now that you're giving this book a skeptical look, maybe try renting out your place when you travel or just when there are big events in town. I know someone who rents out their garage and another who rents out their parking space. Don't need it yet want to keep it just in case? Rent it out. Who knew you could get top dollar for that dismal basement of yours?

2) **Teach a Class at a Gym or Fitness Studio:** This one is a triple winner. Why? Because not only are you getting paid, not only are you getting fit, you're having fun and boosting your confidence! My spin class instructor is actually a full-time real estate agent. She teaches three classes a week and gets her workout in. You can meet new people, make extra money and prevent yourself from skipping exercise when there is moola on the table. Not into the high intensity of group fitness or spin? Try yoga, water aerobics or dance. There is demand for instructors of all levels. Whatever makes your heart (and back, hips, etc.) happy.

3) **Sell Your Expertise:** Can you design websites? Are you good at writing essays? Tutoring math? Passionate about any subject where there is an audience? On sites such as *SkillShare* online learning, you can teach online classes and get paid every time a student takes your class. Also, you can teach courses on sites like Udemy or post videos to YouTube. I can't tell you how many times I have to beg my techy friends to help me fix my website or some other IT issue. Not into tech? Maybe you're good at painting, landscape architecture or event logistics. If you want to just do these things for extra cash when you feel like it,

that's the best part of being a freelance worker. *Fiverr* and *Freelancer.com* are your friends.

4) **Sell Unused Items:** Now, this isn't a sustainable strategy. I don't want to hear about readers who sold their belongings and now sleep on the floor or have one drinking glass at their place. This is for someone who feels as if they need a jump start and have the inventory to detach from. Have you used that tent in the last five years? When was the last time you needed all six of your suitcases? Or how about that patio furniture that you never use anymore? If you found yourself buying things on impulse, or gave up an activity that requires gear, you may want to think about getting rid of it to boost your cash cushion. These days, you can pretty much rent anything you need, from snow-boards to bikes to firepits. Don't believe me? Check out places like Home Depot, your public library and REI for all the cool things you can rent, and you'll stand there in awe at why you ever bought all that stuff.

5) **Start a Side Business:** This doesn't have to be anything extravagant where you need to get a patent or register an LLC. Maybe you love gardening or training pets. Maybe you love making jams and

sauces, so try your hand at the farmer's market. Or maybe you like making jewelry, wedding photography, or making custom canvas wall art. There are people who will pay you for that. Surely there are local trade shows or festivals to test your product and show off your talent. Or test out your market by giving or sharing your product with friends and family. Then you can gauge the level of interest in the general marketplace. For example, you love to bake, so you create a custom cookie platter for a barbecue with your logo on napkins. Not only do you fulfill your part in bringing something, it's free publicity!

Five Apps to Use that can Help You Make Money

By the time you read this, I'm sure that more apps will come onto the scene that can help you make more money with relative ease and flexibility. The purpose of this chapter is to help you think outside of the box to earn more money. Maybe you only have free time on Wednesday nights. Maybe you didn't know you could merge your hobbies with something that earns money, such as walking dogs for *Rover*. With just a little effort, you can start accumulating cash to reach short-term and eventually long-term financial goals.

1) **Idle:** This app is a triple win, because you can rent things you don't use that often (avoiding unnecessary purchases), you can post items you own for rent, and it helps wean our society off the soul sucking trap of consumerism and overconsumption, helping preserve our natural resources. That tent you bought and used over Fourth of July weekend? Rent it out! Or how about that snowboard you haven't yet sold? On the other side, let's say you need a center sound speaker for a house party or a canopy for a family reunion. You can find almost anything you need on the app. I have seen

things such as slow cookers and buffet platters being rented, so think outside the box and earn some extra bucks!

2) **Turo:** Okay, so you're tired of hearing how everyone and their mom is earning extra bucks driving for Uber these days and you're not about to be someone's Friday night babysitter/chauffeur. Well, now you can just rent your car out! This one is a little risky in my eyes, as you never know how someone is going to treat your car, whether it's flooring it across the onramp or slamming on the brakes continuously. But if you don't mind that, or the car is old leased or something (check your contract first) Turo might be for you. For people who have multiple vehicles or live in the city and rarely use it, Turo can be one of those tools to help you earn extra cash without much work.

3) **Airbnb:** Okay, I know, someone hit the *obviously* button! But if you think about all the side-hustles out there, Airbnb is the one with the most return, with average monthly incomes of around $900-$1000 per month. Not bad for renting out a spare bedroom, vacation condo or a furnished basement! I was a little leery on trying it as a host but found that Airbnb does a good job of screening

and letting the host customize their guidelines so that it is clear upfront. The nice thing about Airbnb is if your guest is a little obnoxious, they are usually gone within a few days and then you can change your criteria. On the other hand, I know of people who rent their rooms to foreign students or workers long term and completely regret how they jumped into the deal just a week or two in.

4) **Dolly:** This is a new one I found out about, but I'll tell you, it's a lifesaver. I had to move my bed across downtown, about a mile away to my new place. Rather than going through the hassle of hiring movers or renting a truck, Dolly is an easy to use app that gave me an estimate of what I needed done, and then someone came just a few hours later. It cost about $70, but unless you have friends with trucks who owe you favors, it could have been much more. Speaking of having a truck, if you have a pickup, cargo van or trailer, you can sign up on the app and decide which jobs you want to take on through the app and earn some extra money rather than watching a rerun of Seinfeld for the twelfth time. Even if you don't have a vehicle for Dolly purposes, you can help with just manual labor and make $15 an hour or more, according to the app.

5) **DeCluttr:** Okay, this one is for all you hoarders or wannabe minimalists. Let's say you've accumulated your fair share of stuff be it books or your Xbox. Rather than posting each one on Craigslist or holding a garage (or porch) sale, you can simply use this app to list your items, see if and what it qualifies for, pack it in a box and send it off to them. Not only are you cleaning out your life and getting organized, you're making money and giving your possessions a second life. Now they probably won't accept great aunt Margery's cookie tins, but some things are better left donated or passed on to your cousins.

Five of the Best
Birthday Freebies so Far

Okay, so this won't exactly save you money on a recurring basis, but why not save money and get spoiled on your big day without guilting someone else into it? You can even get freebies for an anniversary or special days for the company providing the rewards program. Wouldn't you rather get tons of free food, drinks, and treats, rather than buying them yourself? A simple Google search will serve you well. Here are some tips to get you started.

1) **Check Locally:** Some of the best birthday freebies depend on where the business is located. I've seen some places that are not chains offer the best perks, such as free dinner, a massage, or a round of golf. Think about your favorite restaurants, entertainment venues and bakeries. One of my favorite restaurants in Denver provides free dessert for you AND your guests on your birthday, even if you don't eat there. And it's their only location, not a chain. Or **Sprinkles Cupcakes**, mainly in sunny CA, which offers a free cupcake. Remember to look for ones where you don't have to make a purchase or have to use them on your actual birthday. (Let's hope you are loved enough that

someone takes you out!) Usually this requires signing up for a loyalty club.

2) **Nothing Bundt Cakes:** Who doesn't love a charming little Bundt cake? Well, if you don't, it's always a nice surprise for that special someone or to earn brownie points with a colleague at work. Walk in, show the email and walk out with a bundtlet. Plus, they usually have free samples of the hot new flavor.

3) **IHOP:** I've pretty much have forgotten about this one, particularly because I don't find their food healthy and don't live near one. However, if you're a pancake fan, you're in luck. They offer a free stack of pancakes of their rooty-tooty pancakes.

4) **Pinkberry:** Free frozen yogurt! You can enjoy it topped with some fresh kiwi or sliced almonds and feel less guilty than downing some ice cream. (Side note, **Ben and Jerry's** and **Baskin Robbins** also offer a free ice cream cone for your birthday.)

5) **Red Robin:** If you've had your sugar high and want some real food, you can get a free burger at this place, and then once you're done, top it off with your free **Starbucks** reward (which you can use for

food, too). Want more ideas? Check out this article or do a simple Google search on *birthday freebies.* https://www.retailmenot.com/blog/birthday-free-bies.html

Five Ways to Effectively Donate to Charity

I hope I've made it abundantly clear how noble it is to include charitable giving into your life. If you're lucky enough to buy a home, go on vacations and enjoy nice dinners or have the latest and greatest gadgets, you're in a prime position to donate. Think of everything that makes our society wonderful. There is likely a charitable endeavor behind it. Like to hike? There's probably a local Land Trust behind trail construction and ongoing preservation efforts. Giving also makes us better people, more compassionate, connected, happy and optimistic about all the great people and efforts out there.

1) **<u>Verify the Charity:</u>** This is probably the most important step. Not only do you want to ensure that your charity is an IRS recognized organization in good standing, but also that it does not have any scandals or transparency issues affecting it. Use sites such as *charitynavigator.org* to analyze how well the charities you are interested in run the business aspects, including accounting and the percent of donations that actually go to the programs. The last thing you want is to muster up the courage to donate, only to realize pennies on the

dollar actually went to helping the program recipients. Look at the ratings and read about the experience of others. Research the charity on the news. Make sure you feel confident about to whom you are giving your hard-earned dollars.

2) **Avoid Solicited Phone/Mail Campaigns:** Some of these are legitimate. (I've struck up a conversation with my alma mater's fundraising staff on occasion, although I kindly asked to be taken off the list.) Much of the time, though, if someone is calling asking for donations, they probably aren't legitimate. Even so, you don't have enough time to do your due diligence on the charity or if it aligns with your values right when someone calls. If you get something in the mail from a charity you haven't heard of or supported in the past, are they really effectively using your donation? It costs a good bundle to hire staff to manage the mailing list, send out letters and apply postage, and they may even offer you a free gift. It's best to find out what charities you want to support (and are effective, see tip #1) and then support them monthly or annually. Ask them to take your name off their solicitation list or at least limit it to email only.

3) **Consider a Donor Advised Fund (DAF):** Now if you're really altruistic and well-heeled, a DAF (also known as a Giving Fund) can be an excellent tool to maximize your giving and also make it less burdensome on you. It's an account where you can put cash or securities in it to be invested or granted to charities of your choosing. The funds in a DAF grow tax-free, and they take care of all the paperwork so there's no need to track checks and receipts. Let's say you inherited Boeing stock from Great Grandma Phyllis years ago. Instead of using your own after-tax income to make your charitable donations, you can donate the stock and there are no capital gains to you. You can also spread the proceeds of it among different charities and over different years. A DAF also offers continuity. If you get a windfall or sell an investment property and have high income, you can throw a chunk of it into your DAF and give grants over five years instead of a gift all at once.

4) **Check into Employer Matching Programs:** Many employers offer matching programs to their employees, either year-round or during special giving events such as the holidays. A friend of mine works for a company who allows them to have payroll deductions or a percentage of their bonus taken

out and given to their charity of choice. Another company that serves higher education gives a matching donation for any donation given to a K-12 or higher education institution. Keep an eye out for company newsletters or ask an HR colleague about charitable giving benefits. If nothing is available, keep in mind that many charities participate in events such as Giving Tuesday, and whatever donations they receive during that timeframe will be matched by their respective benefactors.

5) **Sometimes Volunteering is Worth More:** If you don't have enough discretionary income, volunteers are often just as much, if not more valued than donations. Ask any business owner and they'll say their biggest expense is payroll. Many organizations, such as advocacy or civil rights groups, may need dollars more than volunteers to purchase marketing exposure or pay their attorneys to pursue lawsuits, so don't be discouraged. Many groups need volunteers, whether it is directly for their programs (tutoring low income children or cleaning up a riverbed) or for their fundraising efforts (sending out mailers or creating content for social media campaigns).

Five Things to Know before Executing Your Business Idea

Starting a business is serious business. Before you quit your job to open a luxury car wash, test out your business idea to logically evaluate if you are making a prudent decision before jumping in with both feet. Business validation, finding a mentor and executing with confidence is key.

1) **An Idea does not Equal a Viable Business:** Sure, you might have an innovative, mind-blowing idea for an app that can change the way graduate students collaborate on their work, but is it commercially viable? How will you actually earn money, and why would people pay you for it or choose to advertise with you? Any successful business owner does their due diligence on why people would do business with them and if the business can support itself through various market cycles, competitors, and changes in supply chain. Also, you may be exceptionally good at raising money, cash management and hiring bright people, but if those employees aren't as enthusiastic about your product as you are, none of that will matter.

2) <u>**You Don't have to Come Up with Something Edgy and New:**</u> Many of us have shaken our heads, thinking, "Why didn't I think of that?" When we learn about a new product or service gaining fierce popularity (Thanks, nut butter squeeze packs), we wish we would have thought of it. However, many entrepreneurs have found success by simply improving upon an existing business model. I have seen this with fast-casual healthy eateries, limo companies, marketing companies and even delivery services. Many creative folks have a lightbulb moment when standing in line or riding their bike and run into frustration that translates into, "I can do this better." Look at where you spend your money and what you would improve on.

3) <u>**Write and Solicit Feedback on a Business Plan:**</u> This point is so crucial. Many excellent business concepts start with a bang and then falter because they didn't plan on how to deal with logistical nightmares, supplier shortfalls or where to direct their niche marketing efforts. Writing a business plan will force you to identify risks, opportunities and strengths and weaknesses about your business concept. It also prompts you to think critically about the viability of your idea in the face of

numerous risks businesses face in ever-changing economies, technologies, and consumer preferences. When you're finished writing it, seek feedback on it. You would be surprised to find out about things you didn't consider that could run you into the ground, or a method of appealing to an unlikely customer base simply by asking someone with different experience or tastes than your own.

4) **Facilitate Relationships with Advisors or Mentors:** Building on the last point, you must seek feedback and advice from others who have either been in your shoes or have relevant experience in areas with which you may not be as familiar. If you're thinking of opening a bakery, seek advice from someone who is not in direct competition with you and has been in successful operation for some time. This can be a family member, a connection on LinkedIn, a member of your alumni group or a member of your local small business association or chamber of commerce. They'll read over your business plan, provide counsel on cash flow or HR issues and will help you identify opportunities to strategically expand or draw more business your way. Ask any successful entrepreneur, and they likely had one or more mentors/advisors coaching

them from the very beginning. Be respectful and be persistent!

5) **Learn from the Mistakes of Others before You:**
This can somewhat be accomplished by consulting with your mentors, but also seek this information out on your own. When reading up online, you can often find articles, forums or interviews on what some business owners wish they had done differently or what led to struggles or failures in their endeavors. Not everyone who has failed will be candid, and many will blame various factors, so using your judgement here is key. When they failed, did they turn it around or did it lead to bankruptcy? How did they learn from their mistakes? How did they turn around and apply what they'd learned? For example, you may think doing your own social media marketing will save you money, but maybe someone else did that and it didn't work out. Instead, they used a freelance referral to do it for them so they can focus more on running the business. Thus, now their sales have tripled!

Five Ways to
Raise Money for Your Business

So you've come up with a groundbreaking idea, run some validation and written a business plan. Now--where to get the money to execute? Unless you're well-connected, you'll need to get creative with a mix of the tips below to get your idea off the ground.

1) **Use a Crowdfunding Website:** Leverage the opportunities technology provides you. Twenty years ago, it probably would have been very difficult to raise money from strangers, let alone online. Now, you have sites like *Kickstarter*, *GoFundMe* and others that allow you to share your vision with the world and raise funds in a matter of days. You list your project, such as raising $50,000 for a documentary you want to make and share your passionate story with donors. In return for being a part of your project and supporting it, you might invite them to a free VIP screening or include them in the credits. It's like pitching to a venture capitalist firm, but you're pitching to the world of the Internet. As mentioned in the masterful 2015 book *Bold* by Peter Diamandis and Steven Kotler, some tips for success include:

- Creating early excitement (scarcity among prizes helps, too)
- Budgeting 10% margin for platform fees and cost of rewards in your target
- Targeting for a fundraising period of 33-40 days
- Perks valued at $25 are the single most claimed reward

2) **Attend a Startup Week Event:** More than ever, these events are sprouting up in cities around the country. Denver, where I currently reside, has one of the largest startup week events in the fall, and it is free for anyone to attend. These events are a goldmine, because even if you don't get the chance to pitch your idea in front of a panel, it's an excellent opportunity to network with like-minded entrepreneurs, mentors, philanthropists and venture capitalists. The sessions are incredibly dense with useful information and perspectives, as well. Search for a startup week event near you and see if there are volunteer positions available, or just ask the organizers if you can help. This gives you an alternate perspective and perhaps access to individuals you may not normally have. You never know to whom you'll be pitching and the connections they might have. Can't attend in

person? Check out the website or YouTube for recorded sessions.

3) **Pitch to an Angel Investor:** So, let's say you don't get the chance to pitch in front of venture capitalists in some glass tower in NYC. Startup events are great places to apply and pitch your idea. Try to find angel investors in your area to whom you can pitch. www.angelinvestmentnetwork.us is one of the current sites where you can use to find angel investors in your area, along with a simple Google search for *Angel Investors [my city]*. There are clubs and Meetup groups around the world that fit this kind of shoe. When you get the chance, make sure you are over-prepared. Know your numbers, how much you need, have a compelling story and anticipate their concerns or questions. Always be one step ahead, as you've got to stand out among all the other pitches and really move them so that they hand over money to you.

4) **Get an SBA Loan:** Another perk of living in this great country is we have resources like the US Small Business Association, whose mission is to aid, counsel and support the interests of small business owners. They have wonderfully helpful resources on their website, including how to write

a business plan and employ marketing strategies, among other topics to help you succeed. Thus, they also offer loans guaranteed by the SBA and will counsel you and help find a lender that will be the best fit for you. They also may be able to help you find lower rates and more competitive terms than generally available through other lenders.

5) **Offer Equity to a Business Partner:** Some of this is already implied in the fact that if you pitch to investors, they will want a piece of the action, known as equity in the business in exchange for an upfront investment. This can take a number of forms. Maybe you know an old college friend who knows how to code really well, and you have an idea for an app. Or perhaps you know of a friend, family member, mentor or some connection who either has connections themselves, or has some startup funds and might be interested in investing with you. Many successful startups started out as a team. Think about who might master the skills that complement you, be it public speaking, programming, marketing or negotiating, and consider discussing your business idea with them to see if they want to go in with you. As always, be sure to protect yourself and formally enter into a partnership that defines who owns what and the role of

each, to reduce the chances of any souring of the relationship or legal battles.

Five Ways being Organized will Save You Money

I'll just leave you with this. If you're not organized, it is going to cost you one way or another. Responsible habits, productive routines, and repeatable systems for the way you run your life will be a substantial boost to your financial wellbeing. If you constantly misplace bills, forget invoice due dates, or lose gift cards, get organized!

1) **Time is Money:** Simply put, if you're not organized, you're going to spend more time searching for things. Keys, bills, passwords, you name it. Time is the finite resource each of us has, so why waste it being frustrated and scurrying around trying to find things all the time? You could be enjoying time with friends, reading, meditating, cooking and whatever else you invest your time in that matters to you. Further, if you're constantly spending time searching for things, you may be late to work, miss a flight or have to buy your partner in crime an extra special birthday present for being late to their surprise bash. Put things where they belong, make a spreadsheet, automate your bills and develop a system to rid your life of clutter and

disorganization. You'll be surprised how at ease you'll feel by worrying that much less about things in your life.

2) **Gift Cards and Cash can't be Replaced:** Sure, you can call up your credit card company and get the card replaced, usually for free. You can get a new badge for work and ask the library for a new card, as well. What about those things that you can't get back? A $100 gift card from your aunt or cash given to you by friends after you booked concert tickets for everyone? I shake my head when I see some of my friends scatter cash on their dresser, leave bills in pockets or center consoles, or accidentally put money somewhere and then forget it. Or imagine you lose your driver's license or passport? Not only is that going to cost you money, it'll cost you time and sanity going through the process of applying for a new one. And it'll cost more if it makes you miss a flight! Keeping things like these in a safe or a little box in your closet where you know you keep items of importance will help.

3) **Protect Yourself in an Emergency:** Let's say you get into a minor car accident, and whoops--where is the insurance card? Oh I forgot to take pictures! Or maybe an HVAC contractor did faulty work and

your heater goes out in the dead of winter. What are you going to do when you call the company and don't have a copy of the warranty of what work was completed? Are you going to argue with them or just have someone come out right away, so your family doesn't freeze? In my own experience, I forgot the code to my new bike lock and had to cut it so I could get to an appointment on time. Do yourself a favor and keep important documents in a file on your desk or closet, or better yet, scan in receipts and other documents to Google Drive, a spreadsheet or cloud that you can access on the spot.

4) **"Do You have any Proof of That?"** In the society we live in today where trust has frayed, the customer is no longer always right and we must have everything documented, it pays to keep tabs on your money. Let's say you buy a surround sound system online and a month later it stops working. What happened to the receipt? Or you ordered $100 worth of takeout for your book club dinner and they messed up the order, so you had to go buy more food. If you have the receipt, you can get a refund. Apart from receipts, invoices, and warranty information, it's a good idea to have correspondence via email or a recorded call, as

well. If an associate told you they would price match a service, extend an expired discount or waive a fee to gain your business, it will be that much easier to get what you want if you have documented proof of these promises and interactions.

5) **Buying Things that You Thought You Lost/Ran Out Of:** I've done this more times I care to admit before I got serious about organization. Out of berries and avocados? Oops, I just bought more. Now I'll have to eat more than I intended or toss it. Or what about when you throw a party and buy chicken or specialty desserts and now you have to throw them out because you have no room in your freezer? Even if this applies to non-perishables such as olive oil or body wash, you may be more generous in using it up since you now have an abundance. Maybe you lost your headphones when they were just in your gym bag or figured your watch is long gone, so you buy another one and realize your old watch was in the pocket of your cooler bag. Make a habit of cleaning out bags and pockets every day and deep clean closets, drawers, and other storage areas at least monthly. Always remember the saying, "A place for everything and everything in its place."

Five Habits to Develop to Jumpstart a Lifetime of Financial Success

So throughout the course of this book I have showered you with tons and tons and *tons* of ways to save money, earn money and find more fulfillment in life without having to pull out a credit card every time. Now I leave you with recommendations based on my own experience learning online and networking with successful people to ask them, *what makes them successful?* Sure, you've rolled your eyes at the fact that they wake up at 4am to meditate, work out and save the world before we've even hit the snooze button. However, if you really want lifelong financial acumen, take note.

1) **Manage Your Time:** Time is the most precious resource we have. You can never get it back. It's one of the few things you and I have in common with the likes of Bill Gates, Mariah Carey or the President of the United States--we all get the same amount of time every day. It's what you do with your time that counts. I'm not going to lecture you to stop watching TV after dinner and instead go sell things online. However, I encourage you to schedule time for things and have a *routine*. We all

need to do things like buy groceries and do laundry, so set a time each week to do these chores. Make Thursday's after dinner *me time* to unwind with your favorite show or whatever you like to do, so you don't feel guilty about it and resent yourself. Schedule your lunchtime at work so you can get the break you need and get back in time to resume your productivity. The idea is to stop wasting time on things that have no value or bring you no enjoyment. *Always live meaningfully.*

2) **Embrace "No":** There are two parts to this. You should let the *no's* other people tell you deflect off you like rain drops. It doesn't cost you anything to ask for something, and every no gets you closer to your next yes! Whether you ask for a raise, pitch to investors or make an offer on a car, getting a *no* is rarely personal rejection. It's just a matter of circumstances. Be okay with it, expect it and have a Plan B. The other part of this point is to learn to say *no* yourself. I have found this is much harder for some people than others, depending on their personalities. Those who crave acceptance and belonging may be more prone to say *yes* to requests for help or to plan the school carnival, when they are already drowning in unopened mail or their marriage is unraveling because they don't

have the time to devote to it. Get very honest with yourself about your life's mission and what is important to you and say no to things that don't match up with that vision.

3) **Get Completely Comfortable with Negotiation:** As I've alluded to earlier, some people get very uncomfortable having to directly negotiate with someone and would rather cave in than deal with the suspense. That's going to cost you in life! So many things that affect our financial success depend on negotiation. Buying a car, a house, or a sofa. Asking for a raise. Negotiating with services such as contractors, vendors, or legal services. Be polite and openminded, and just go into it with the best intent. If you struggle with trying to negotiate, think about the fact that the person across the table may rather you negotiate than just walk away because the deal doesn't work for you. It's all relative. My biggest suggestion to you if you want to get better at negotiation is to read *Never Split the Difference* by Chris Voss. It's loaded with solid advice that I promise will help you!

4) **Value People, not Things:** The most successful people may be able to buy anything they want--except relationships. Get in the habit of valuing the

people in your life, not the material possessions in your life. Invest in your relationships and it will pay dividends throughout your life. If you make people in your life feel like they can count on you, that you value their relationship with you, they will do everything they can to hold up their end of the bargain. I've learned this myself firsthand. For example, when I send a handwritten thank you card to people who have introduced me to others whom I want to meet or get in front of, it pays back in dividends. It has resulted in increased business revenue, job interviews, and special access to events (not to mention copious discounts). How much does a card cost? Maybe a few dollars, but it more than pays for itself. The point to take home is that if you genuinely value others, they will pave the road to success for you.

5) **Take Care of Yourself:** This is a given. If you are burned out, lacking sleep or suffering from health issues, you will never perform at your best. Remove barriers to your optimum performance by controlling the things you can. Get into an exercise routine and keep it interesting so it's sustainable. Learn to cook or at least choose the healthiest, plant-based options when you eat. Sleep six to eight hours a night. When your body is healthy,

you will think clearly and be more productive! Make time to meditate, be mindful of your surroundings and forgive yourself often.

Bonus Section:
The FIRE Movement

Unless you've been living under a rock this year, you've surely heard about the FIRE Movement that's been, well, to put it simply, on fire! FIRE stands for *Financial Independence Retire Early*. It's been featured in numerous blogs and magazines and even PBS, and there was even a big story in the Wall Street Journal. I'm proud to say that the person who is considered by some as the Godfather of the FIRE movement, Pete Adeney (aka Mr. Money Mustache) lives right here in Colorado. He is truly a wise person in this subject matter, having retired at the ripe old age of 30. I would highly encourage you to read his blog or even just search for videos and interviews with his name. Quite frankly, as I write this after Thanksgiving weekend 2019, there is a flurry of various people who have achieved their own version of FIRE and generously provide the how-to steps of how they got there.

In my opinion, this is nothing groundbreaking or new strategies which will get you rich quickly. Rather, it's a trend that is gaining traction due to changes in our working culture. Sure, your parents may have worked for some corporation or municipality for 40 years and are coasting on a pension for the rest of their lives. However, that is not the case for many Americans today. People change jobs more often, they get laid off and start freelancing, jumping into the gig economy or just go back to school to pursue a completely different career. Many people don't feel loyal to their employers anymore due to a variety of reasons, such as lack of job security. On the other hand, many people feel they are burned out or just can't fathom working until their 60's or 70's just to be able to finally kick back, and then they get set back with a health issue. People are waking up to the notion that they don't need to accumulate the big house, SUV and all the new tech by slaving away and not really savoring the present.

We've heard so much about *experiences over material possessions* and this has really caught on. People are realizing, "Hey wait a minute. I'd rather just go for a hike or play with my kid in the park. I don't need to buy a boat and the second house on the lake." They are resorting to a simpler way of life and finding out it can be sustained by several years of sacrifice and massive savings, and then calling it quits early. The book *Your Money or Your Life* by Vickie Robin and Joseph Dominguez first came out in 1992 and really emphasized simple living and the FIRE concept even before it really became a movement. I highly recommend a read. There's a new version out for 2018!

Five Ways to Achieve FIRE Status

So, you've decided you're going to try to jump in the FIRE? (Sorry, too cheesy but too easy!) Well, luckily for you, I have been practicing many concepts of FIRE for a few years now without actually realizing I was a part of this ultra-frugal cult (kidding, but really). I achieved a net worth of over $400,000 by my late 20's without making six figures or even owning real estate. Even if you don't see yourself attaining FIRE status anytime soon, or even if you simply want to retire, the habits below will serve you well in whatever path you choose in life. Remember, FIRE doesn't mean you reach a certain point in your 40's and then stop working, sitting around doing nothing. It is different for each person and essentially just means Financial *Independence*. You can *choose* to do what you want with your time, skills and passions. You don't have to be tied to a director-level job you hate working at 60 hours per week.

1) **Know and Track Your Net Worth:** You've got to write out the blueprints before you build the house. Using resources previously mentioned in this book, such as *mint.com*, you can easily integrate your financial accounts to keep track of your net worth. Knowing your net worth is imperative

to know, since you will be relying, in part at least, on the income derived from the assets that make up your net worth. It's also encouraging to see your net worth increase steadily as you work toward your target number that will enable you to retire. Let's say you need $40,000 per year to live comfortably. If you have an investment portfolio that is generating 6% returns, and you plan to take 4% (counting for inflation and bear markets), you'll want a $1 million portfolio before you can burn all your suits.

2) **Understand Your Cash Flow:** You can't have an idea of how much your monthly savings potential is if you don't know where your income is going. Notice, I didn't say the dreaded word *budget* as if you need to investigate where that $3.20 in cash went last week. Rather, understand where your take-home pay is going in a more fluid sense. Obviously, the big three are housing, transportation and food. Don't look at this as you have to calculate your gas receipts, grocery bills and electricity bills to the penny, but what can you cut out or cut down in each spending category? For example, can you wash your car yourself or take it to the dealer for a free wash? Can you give up your parking spot and park on the street? Even better,

forget using your car and opt to bike, walk or take public transportation. For housing, look at what costs you can cut out. Internet, cable and energy are easy ones. Are you spending too much on heating and cooling? Are you spending colossal amounts on watering your lawn in the summer? Are you buying booze every time you go out to eat? Are you eating lunch out every day? Take a hard look at your necessities and then what you are willing to cut out, so that those dollars can now work toward getting you to financial independence.

3) **Pay Yourself First:** See a recurring theme here? I've mentioned this in my earlier advice about automating your savings. That's what paying yourself first means. Not, "Oh I worked hard this week so I'm going to buy myself a watch before I take care of those pesky bills." No, dear. Pay yourself first, not buy things for yourself first. Get a set amount going into savings, retirement and investment accounts so you don't skip on your progress to FIRE. As you refine your cash flow (see above) and free up more money, you can increase the amounts going into your investment and savings accounts. There are a plethora of apps that will take spare change and invest it for you, and many

financial institutions allow you to set up recurring payments to your accounts with them because, duh, they want your money, too!

4) **Start a Side Hustle:** At a certain point, you can't really cut more of your expenses without living under a bridge, making your car run on three tires or eating nothing but beans and rice. Your upside potential, though, is pretty much unlimited. What is not unlimited is your time, so choose a side hustle carefully. How much can you REALLY make working for Lyft or DoorDash in your free time? You may start off with what you know, such as landscape maintenance or photography. This is completely okay and is encouraged, as long as you feel you are being properly compensated for your time, are enjoying it and it's not wearing you out. Many blogs and financial websites list various side hustles you can do, from those already mentioned to blogging, freelance consulting, selling laundry soap at a farmer's market or renting out your condo on Airbnb. Get creative!

5) **Ask Yourself, "Is it Really Worth It?"** If you are going to be miserable and can't seem to find a way to enjoy life while you are on the journey to financial independence, do some introspection to

determine why you want financial independence in the first place. What will it mean for you? How will you find meaning in your life once you've gotten there? If you are jeopardizing your health, relationships or career development and can't get out from under the cloud, know there is nothing wrong with working into your 60's or 70s. We need workers! Who is going to teach our kids, build our roads, grow our food and service our accounts if we all run toward FIRE? Many people love what they do. I'm sure you've heard the quote, "If you love what you do, you'll never work a day in your life."

Conclusion

You made it! You just read through 65 categories of *Financial Fives*. Congratulations! I hope you are buzzing with excitement on all the things you learned about saving, earning, protecting yourself and more. As I mentioned when we embarked on this journey, I designed this book in a way so as to provide you with concise, yet rich and immediately actionable, content on improving your financial life. You don't have to read 300 pages of some other book, initially feeling empowered, but only a week later struggling to remember three things you learned or implemented.

With *Financial Fives*, you can always refer back to the sections which most apply to your life right now or are most relevant to you. Maybe you're not getting married just yet, but when you pop the question you can pull this book from your collection and refer back to the sections on weddings and financial conversations to have with your partner. Or perhaps you are planning to buy a home in the next few months. Even if you are not planning either of these things, you surely buy groceries and such, so we've got you covered. If you notice in the Table of Contents, every section starts on an odd numbered page. Of course, there surely is another topic that may have been omitted, so let me know! Go to *financialfives.com* and send me a note.

If I can leave you with just one last piece of advice, it's to start somewhere. Approach your boss for a raise. Set up automatic bill pay or regular contributions to your Roth IRA. Do it today! Set a reminder in your phone to implement just one idea from this book on Sunday nights or the first of the month--whatever works for your schedule. Maybe pick a random chapter once per month and vow to implement that advice. Then, share this knowledge with others! Let a friend borrow this book or buy a copy for your nephew who just graduated college. Donate it to your library. Maybe even start a book club and hold your members accountable on what section you are currently debating. What steps are you going to take between now and next week?

It's my sincere hope that this book will allow you to live a life of purpose, fulfillment and financial security. Cut out the fluff from your life, make commitments and stick to your decisions. You are holding personal finance gold. Empower yourself to get your life in order and change your view of money. Thank you for taking the time to read *Financial Fives*. **Be sure to keep in touch at *financialfives.com* and please leave a review to let others know how much you enjoyed it!**

References

Five Ways Zero Waste Will Save You Money:

Strutner, Suzy. "America Has More Self-Storage Facilities Than McDonald's, Because Apparently We're All Hoarders." *HuffPost,* HuffPost, 21 Apr. 2015, www.huffpost.com/entry/self-storage-mcdonalds_n_7107822

Five Adult Conversations to have with Your Parents/Siblings:
Cost of Long-Term Care: *LongTermCare.gov,* 10 Oct. 2017, longtermcare.acl.gov/the-basics

Five Ways to Save at the Grocery Store:
"FSIS." *Food Product Dating,* 14 Dec. 2016, www.fsis.usda.gov/wps/portal/fsis/topics/food-safety-education/get-answers/food-safety-fact-sheets/food-labeling/food-product-dating/food-product-dating.
Dykman, April. "Four Cheap and Healthy Grains." *Get Rich Slowly,* 6 Feb. 2010, www.getrichslowly.org/four-cheap-and-healthy-grains
"Egg Storage: How Long Do Eggs Last?" *Incredible Egg,* www.incredibleegg.org/cooking-school/tips-tricks/egg-storage

Five ways to Improve Your Credit Score:
Dratch, Dana. "7 Ways To Improve Your Credit Score." *Bankrate*, Bankrate.com, 10 Nov. 2017, www.bankrate.com/finance/debt/7-simple-ways-improve-credit-score-1.aspx?ic_id=home_smart%2Bspending_homepage-financial-goals_credit_7-ways-to-improve-your-credit-score

Five Protective Measures to Take While You're Young:
Jarrell, Matthew. "Will vs Trust: Knowing The Difference." *Investopedia*, Investopedia, 18 Feb. 2018, www.investopedia.com/articles/personal-finance/051315/will-vs-trust-difference-between-two.asp

"The Ultimate Gift Experience | MOVIE | DVD | BOOK." *The Ultimate Gift Experience | MOVIE | DVD | BOOK*, 2011, www.theultimategift.com

Five Ways to Save Energy at Home:

"Learn About LED Lighting." *Products | ENERGY STAR*, United States Department of Energy, www.energystar.gov/products/lighting_fans/light_bulbs/learn_about_led_bulbs

"Heating & Cooling." *Department of Energy*, www.energy.gov/heating-cooling

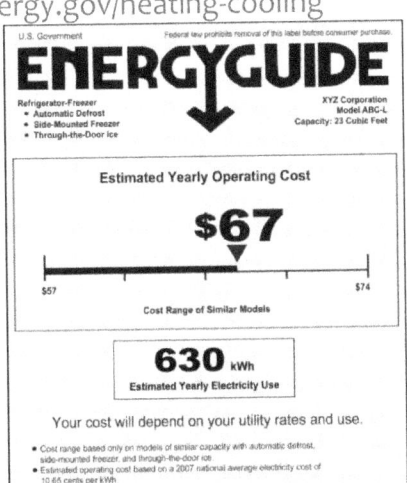

Five Ways to Save on Throwing a Party:

Dratch, Dana. "6 Money-Saving Tips For Summer Parties." *Bankrate*, Bankrate.com, 1 June 2016, www.bankrate.com/finance/frugal/money-saving-tips-summer-parties.aspx#slide=1

Person. "8 Inexpensive Ways to Throw a Kick-Ass Party." *Cosmopolitan*, Cosmopolitan, 6 Oct. 2017, www.cosmopolitan.com/lifestyle/advice/a33877/cheap-ways-throw-a-party/

Five Ways to Save on Taxes:

Bell, Kay, and Kay Bell. "10 Ways Uncle Sam Helps You Save Money." *Bankrate*, Bankrate.com, 14 Oct. 2008, www.bankrate.com/finance/money-guides/10-ways-uncle-sam-helps-you-save-money-2.aspx

O'Shea, Arielle. "Roth IRA Withdrawals: What You Need to Know." *NerdWallet*, NerdWallet, 18 Apr. 2018, www.nerdwallet.com/blog/investing/roth-ira-withdrawal-rules/

Bell, Kay. "Short-Term vs. Long-Term Capital Gains Tax." *NerdWallet*, NerdWallet, 27 July 2018, www.nerdwallet.com/blog/taxes/short-term-capital-gains-vs-long-term-capital-gains/

Garcia, Adrian D. "Is Living In A State With No Income Tax Better Or Worse?" *Bankrate*, Bankrate.com, 27 July 2018, www.bankrate.com/finance/taxes/state-with-no-income-tax-better-or-worse-1.aspx

"Job Search Expenses Can Be Tax Deductible 2017 | Internal Revenue Service." *Internal Revenue Service*, 25 Aug.

2017, www.irs.gov/newsroom/job-search-expenses-can-be-tax-deductible-2017.

Five Things to Look for When Considering a New City:
"2019 Cost of Living Calculator - Cost of Living Comparison Tool." *SmartAsset*, SmartAsset, smartasset.com/mortgage/cost-of-living-calculator

Five Ways to Save Money When Travelling Abroad:

Schwab.com. "5 Ways to Save Money When Traveling Abroad." *Schwab Brokerage*, 14 June 2018, www.schwab.com/insights/personal-finance/5-ways-to-save-money-when-traveling-abroad?cmp=em-QYB

Five Ways to Save on Ski Season:

Walter, Claire. "11 Ways to Save on Lift Tickets in Colorado." *The Know*, The Know, 28 Oct. 2017, theknow.denverpost.com/2017/10/28/save-money-on-ski-lift-tickets/163168/.

Five Apps to Earn More Money:

Howard, Drew. "How Much Money People Are Really Earning from Uber, Airbnb, and 7 More Side Hustles." *LearnVest*, Business Insider, 20 Aug. 2017, www.businessinsider.com/how-much-people-are-earning-from-uber-airbnb-and-other-side-hustles-2017-8

Five Ways to Manage Your Debt:

Nykiel, Teddy. "10 Student Loan Forgiveness, Cancellation and Discharge Programs." *NerdWallet*, NerdWallet, 22 Feb. 2018, www.nerdwallet.com/blog/loans/student-loans/student-loan-forgiveness

Five Mistakes First-Time Homebuyers Make:

Kearns, Deborah. "14 First-Time Homebuyer Mistakes To Avoid." *Bankrate*, Bankrate.com, 11 Dec. 2018, www.bankrate.com/finance/real-estate/first-time-homebuyer-mistakes-1.aspx#slide=6

Folger, Jean. "Pre-Qualified vs. Pre-Approved: What's the Difference?" *Investopedia*, Investopedia, 10 Feb. 2019, www.investopedia.com/articles/basics/07/prequalified-approved.asp

Five Things to Look for in a New City:

Banton, Caroline. "What Is Included in the Cost of Living?" *Investopedia*, Investopedia, 8 Feb. 2019, www.investopedia.com/terms/c/cost-of-living.asp

Five Ways to Save on Your Wedding:

The Knot. "22 Ways to Save Money on Your Wedding." *Theknot.com*, The Knot, 18 Dec. 2018, www.theknot.com/content/ways-to-save-money-on-wedding.

Five Ways to Efficiently Donate to Charity:

Holden. "Tips for Giving Efficiently." *GiveWell*, Nov. 2016, www.givewell.org/about/donate/more-information/tips

5 Adult Conversations to Have with Siblings/Parents:

"How Much Care Will You Need?" *The Basics - Long-Term Care Information*, US Department of Health and Human Services, 10 Oct. 2017, longtermcare.acl.gov/the-basics/how-much-care-will-you-need.html

Five Ways to Save on Utilities:

Gray, Jessica. "18 Clever Ways to Save on Utility Bills and Still Stay Cool This Summer." *The Penny Hoarder*, Https://Www.thepennyhoarder.com/, 23 Aug. 2018, www.thepennyhoarder.com/smart-money/utility-bill-savings

Five Ways to Raise Money for Your Business:

Newlands, Murray. "Where to Meet Angel Investors and How to Pitch Them When You Do." *Entrepreneur*, Entrepreneur, 17 Mar. 2017, www.entrepreneur.com/article/290698

Small Business Administration, www.sba.gov/funding-programs/loans.
Staff, Inc. "10 Ways to Finance Your Business." *Inc.com*, Inc., www.inc.com/guides/2010/07/how-to-finance-your-business.html

Five Ways to Save on Moving:

"Learn How Much It Costs to Hire Movers." *How Much Are Average Moving Costs?*, HomeAdvisor, www.homeadvisor.com/cost/storage-and-organization/hire-a-moving-service

Five Things to Consider for Your Investment Portfolio:

"Best Online Stockbrokers for Beginners of February 2019." *NerdWallet*, NerdWallet, 2 Jan. 2018, www.nerd-wallet.com/blog/investing/the-best-online-brokers-for-beginners/?trk=nw_gn_4.0

Five Things to Know before Executing Your Business Idea:

Pike, David. "How to Validate Your Business Idea." *StartupNation*, StartupNation Media Group, 22 May 2018, startupnation.com/start-your-business/validate-business-idea

www.ingramcontent.com/pod-product-compliance
Lightning Source LLC
Chambersburg PA
CBHW070525220526
45467CB00003B/860